The Fourth Dimension

V

The Fourth Dimension

Interviews With Christa Wolf

◆

Translated by
HILARY PILKINGTON
(Material Word)

With an Introduction by
KARIN McPHERSON

VERSO

London · New York

First published in 1987 by Heinrich Luchterhand Verlag, Darmstadt and Neuwied, as part of *Christa Wolf: Die Dimension des Autors. Essays und Aufsätze, Reden und Gespräche, 1959–1985.*

This edition published by Verso 1988
© 1987 Luchterhand Verlag
This translation © 1988 Verso

Verso
UK: 6 Meard Street, London W1V 3HR
USA: 29 West 35th Street, New York, NY 10001-2291

Verso is the imprint of New Left Books

British Library Cataloguing in Publication Data
Wolf, Christa, *1929–*
    The fourth dimension: interviews with
    Christa Wolf.
    1. Fiction in German. Wolf, Christa, 1929–
    Critical studies
    I. Title   II. Pilkington, Hilary
    833'.914

    ISBN 0-86091-227-2
    ISBN 0-86091-939-0 Pbk

US Library of Congress Cataloging in Publication Data
Wolf, Christa.
        [Dimension des Autors. English]
        The fourth dimension: interviews with Christa Wolf / translated by
    Hilary Pilkington (material word); with an introduction by Karin
    McPherson.
        p.   cm.
        Revised translation of: Die Dimension des Autors.
        ISBN 0-86091-227-2: $35.00 (U.S.). ISBN 0-86091-939-0 (pbk.):
    $13.95 (U.S.)
        I. Title.
        PT2685.036A26 1988
    833'.914--dc19

Typeset by Leaper & Gard Ltd, Bristol
Printed in Great Britain by Bookcraft (Bath) Ltd, Midsomer Norton, Avon

Contents

ACKNOWLEDGEMENT

The translator would like to acknowledge the assistance of her colleagues Chris Turner and Stuart McKinnon-Evans from the Birmingham-based co-operative Material Word.

CHRISTA WOLF
– AN INTRODUCTION

Karin McPherson

Christa Wolf's reputation as a leading contemporary writer reaches far beyond the boundaries of the German Democratic Republic, the country where her roots lie and to which she remains committed. Born on 18 March 1929 in Landsberg, a small town east of the Oder (now Gorzów Wielkopolski in Poland), at the age of sixteen she was uprooted, like so many of her generation, when she fled with her family from the advancing Soviet army and was resettled by chance, not design, in Mecklenburg, which became part of the GDR at its foundation in 1949. This was also the year in which she entered university and applied for membership of the Socialist Unity Party (SED), following her first encounter with Marxist writing which had a profound effect on her. From 1949 to 1953 she studied German and Philosophy at Jena and Leipzig; in 1951, she married Gerhard Wolf, who, like Christa, is a critic, editor and writer. They have two daughters, born in 1952 and 1956. Christa began her professional career as a critic and literary editor in 1953 in Berlin, where she worked for the Writers' Union under its first president Anna Seghers, whom Wolf adopted as her mentor. She became a member of the Executive Committee in 1955; from 1958 to 1959 she was editor of the literary magazine *Neue Deutsche Literatur*, for which she reviewed contemporary novels; and she was briefly chief editor for the publisher *Neues Leben*. In 1955 she made the first of a number of journeys to the Soviet Union, and this was reflected in her first short narrative prose fiction *Moscow Novella* (1961).

In her early years as a critic and writer, Christa Wolf's political and ideological commitment to the new state and society was at its most affirmative, by contrast with the conflicts between arts and politics of later years. She endorsed the doctrines of Socialist Realism, pronounced by the First Party Secretary Walter Ulbricht in 1951 as binding for contemporary writing in the GDR. Wolf followed the directives given at the Bitterfeld

Conference in 1959, that literary works should reflect the experience of workers in factories and in agriculture, and that writers should gain such experience at first hand. From 1959 to 1962, Wolf lived with her family in the industrial town of Halle, and her six months' experience of work in a railway factory became the basis for her second narrative fictional prose work, *Divided Heaven* (1963). For this she received the Heinrich Mann Prize in 1963, and the National Prize, Third Class in 1964, after the book was filmed by DEFA, the national film company.

In 1962, the Wolfs moved back to Berlin, and have lived there ever since, though in more recent years they have also created a home for themselves in Mecklenburg, the province bordering on the Baltic Sea. By the mid-1960s, Wolf's career as a writer had successfully taken off. Her active political engagement in these years is reflected in her candidature for the Central Committee of the SED between 1963 and 1967. But at the second Bitterfeld Conference of 1964, and at the Writers' Congress of 1965 – at which Socialist Realist principles were once again strictly reinforced – Wolf opened herself to criticism with her warning that literature could not afford to disregard the individuality and personal experience of authors and literary figures. At the Sixth Party Congress of the SED in 1969 her next major fictional prose work, *The Quest for Christa T.* (1968), written in this spirit, was severely criticised and her candidature for the Central Committee not renewed. Notwithstanding her political position, the late 1960s and early 1970s are among Wolf's most productive years as a writer of essays and shorter fiction.

The change of Party Leadership from Ulbricht to Erich Honecker in 1971 marked a change in the cultural climate in the GDR, not least because of improvements in diplomatic relations with the Federal Republic after the signing of the Basic Treaty in 1971, which was followed by recognition of the GDR by a number of Western countries. In a speech at the Fourth Plenary Session of the SED in 1972, Honecker proclaimed that given the consolidated basis of socialism in the GDR there could be no more taboos in respect of the arts in general and literature in particular, with regard either to form or to subject matter. Although the Sixth Plenary of 1972 retracted the spirit of Honecker's speech, the famous Seventh Writers' Congress of 1973 brought a candid reappraisal of past developments in the arts, with contributions by all leading writers – including Christa Wolf. The change was manifest, too, in a wave of publication of works which could not have appeared earlier. Among these were Wolf's essays *The Reader and the Writer* (1971) and the long overdue second edition of *The Quest for Christa T.* (1972).

Largely as a result of the improved international status of the GDR and of her own recognition within her country, Wolf began to travel widely in the West during the 1970s (though during the 1960s she had paid visits to the Federal Republic). In 1974, the Wolfs spent six months in the USA, where Christa Wolf was Max Kade German Writer-in-Residence at Oberlin College, Ohio. In 1978, as part of an increasing programme of lecturing abroad, she gave lectures in Britain and attended the International PEN Meeting in Stockholm.

During the early 1970s, Wolf wrote her major, partly autobiographical, novel about a childhood under National Socialism, A Model Childhood (1976). This shed light on the identity crisis of a whole generation, and appealed equally to readers in both East and West Germany. After the publication of this book, though not as a direct result of its treatment of the past, relations with cultural and political authorities in the GDR once again became strained. The Wolfs, together with a number of other leading writers and artists, signed an open letter petitioning the government to reconsider the step taken against Wolf Biermann, a writer of political songs. Biermann, a communist who had chosen to live in the GDR, albeit under house arrest since the mid-60s, had been refused re-entry after giving a public concert in the Federal Republic. The letter, which was sent to leading newspapers in both West and East Germany, was published only in the West; in the East, the signatories faced charges of disloyalty to the state.

Christa Wolf was reprimanded by the Writers' Union and in 1977 lost her place on the Executive, while Gerhard Wolf lost membership of both the Writers' Union and the Party. As a consequence of these events, a number of writers and artists to whom the Wolfs had been close – among them Sarah Kirsch and Günter Kunert – took up residence in the FRG. The late 1970s are marked by an acute sense of isolation on Christa Wolf's part. She turned to the subject of outsiders in a literary society of an earlier age, the period of Romanticism, in two long essays and a short prose fiction No Place On Earth (1979). Nevertheless, Wolf's recognition abroad, particularly in the German-speaking countries, continued to increase, and she was awarded a number of prestigious prizes. Among these were the West German Georg Büchner Prize in 1980; the Schiller Memorial Prize in 1983; the Austrian State Prize for Literature in 1983; and more recently the Geschwister Scholl Prize in Munich in 1987.

This international recognition is but a reflection of the fact that in recent years Wolf has increasingly turned her attention to issues which are of European, even of worldwide, significance: issues concerning women – through feminist movements, through the development of socialism, and through concern about the nuclear arms race. These issues are all inter-related for Christa Wolf, as she stressed in her contribution to the Encounter for the Advancement of Peace (Berliner Begegnung zur Friedens-förderung) held in December 1981 at the Academy of Arts in Berlin (East). This event, chaired by Stephan Hermlin, was attended by writers, scientists and politicians from both Germanies and from other European countries.

Wolf, one of few women present, claimed that the moribund and self-destructive state in which civilization finds itself is attributable to women's exclusion from the creation of cultural values; that women's voices have been stifled over three thousand years – from the very beginnings of a patriarchal literary tradition in Homer's epics. In her work *Cassandra. A Novel and Four Essays* (1983) Wolf counters this tradition by giving a voice to a woman figure who has previously been silent. In the essays preceding the story of Cassandra, which Wolf first delivered as lectures in 1982 when guest to the Chair of Poetics at Frankfurt in West Germany, she makes public her views on women and on unilateral disarmament. Writing as a means of opening up to public debate issues of urgent political and social concern is Christa Wolf's outstanding contribution of the 1980s. Her latest work *Störfall (Accident*, to be published by Virago in April 1989) was written in July 1986 in direct response to Chernobyl. Taking the form of a diary, this book was published in September 1986 simultaneously in East and West Germany. The award of the National Prize, First Class by the GDR Academy of Arts, of which Wolf has been a long-standing member, is an indication that her leading status as a writer has at last been publicly acknowledged in the GDR.

Christa Wolf's narrative genre is prose in its widest sense. In her thirty years as a writer, she has never tried her hand at poetry or drama, though she was written three film scripts. One of the literary figures to whom she feels a strong affinity, the early nineteenth-century poet Karoline von Günderrode, wrote plays and poetry. Yet in Christa Wolf's interpretation of this historical figure, the adherence to the exacting norms of established (male) literary genres caused Günderrode deep conflict with her need to find fulfilment as a woman.

Writing prose takes on a new meaning for Christa Wolf after the completion of her first two works of fiction, *Moskauer Novelle* (1961) and *Der geteilte Himmel (Divided Heaven)* (1963). In 1968 after completing *The Quest for Christa T.*, her major work of the second half of the 1960s, she wrote a seminal essay *Lesen und Schreiben* (translated as *The Reader and the Writer*, but literally *Reading and Writing*) which, together with a number of other essays, was not published until 1972. In the title essay of this collecton, Christa Wolf reveals that her approach to writing underwent fundamental changes during the first decade of her work as a writer and critic. She redefines prose as a subjective process of 'finding oneself', which she sets in parallel with developments in the socialist society of which she continues to regard herself as an integral part.

She now rejects the notion held previously by herself and other writers who adhered to Socialist Realist theories, that the writer is simply a mirror in which reality is reflected in its meaningful (partisan) totality. This concept of realism is derived from the literary theories of Georg Lukács, who had a strong influence on the theory and practice of writing in the GDR throughout the 1950s. In her essay, Wolf denounces the criteria to which she herself had adhered as a literary critic and editor of East German literature in the 1950s: the linear plot (*Fabel*); the two-dimensional characters (types); the superimposed idea which led to a mechanical process of creating fiction in the guise of objective reality. Instead, Wolf claims that 'prose must seize upon a new reality in a new way, ... must overcome a mechanical attitude to the world in favour of a dialectical one' in which changes are effected through the author's moral sense and vision. Taking as her example the nineteenth-century 'poet, natural scientist and revolutionary' Georg Büchner – whom she regards as the inventor par excellence of modern prose – Wolf demonstrates how Büchner achieves a new reality by transforming an apparently 'objective' piece of documentary writing – Pastor Oberlin's report of the gradual mental breakdown of the eighteenth century poet Lenz – into modern prose by merging his own life experience with that of the documented figure.

Wolf stresses that, for the author, writing here becomes an integral part of the process of living: he/she no longer writes in a detached, 'objective' manner. The mark of modern prose is the constant shift from the third to the first person, from the he/she to the I: this is a feature of almost all Christa Wolf's fictional prose from this point onwards. Through Büchner she discovers the essential 'fourth' dimension of writing and calls it 'depth'. This comprises memory, fantasy and social or moral conscious-ness as integral parts of the author's 'experience'. Not only does this experience enable the writer to create 'reality' in a new and deeper sense (measured against a mere two-dimensional reflection of objective facts); it also establishes the essential link with the society in which he/she lives. Whereas in Socialist Realist prose in its dogmatic definition of the 1950s the author disappeared behind his/her narrative, Wolf now establishes the presence of the author as an individual – as the basic condition without which prose in the modern world, ruled as it is by science, technology and the media, can no longer stake its claim.

At this stage of her development, Wolf does not yet see an unbridgeable rift between the scientist and the writer, as she does in her later works: in fact, she compares writing with the process of scientific discovery in physics. Einstein's Theory of Relativity did for the physical world what Wolf claims for the spiritual realm: it created the break with established concepts of space and time. Both share a need for 'fantastic accuracy' and projection into the future through vision and 'invention'. But this is where the affinity with the natural sciences ends for Christa Wolf, who claims that the writer is bound by 'a truth outside the important world of facts'.

The writer, in her eyes, has one essential advantage over the scientist:

> The narrator can know and make use of the results of science, but what he himself discovers in his search for the nature of man living in society can probably be regarded as 'true' without the need to prove its 'correctness' which every conclusion in natural science demands. (*Reading and Writing*)

The search for truth of this kind has become the centre of Wolf's narrative quest. In her essay *Selbstinterview* (*Interview with Myself*), written in 1966 before *The Quest for Christa T.* was completed, she defends her new approach to reality and (documentary and inner) truth against imagined but plausible criticisms of the book. She claims to have no 'subject matter', no 'plot' or 'milieu' for her latest work; rather, a subjective experience – her incomprehension of the death of a (female) friend – has provided her with the motivation for writing. In this process she combines her own memories, the memories of others documentary material, and 'diaries, letters, sketches' left behind by her friend, into a new type of writing easily recognizable as a form of stream-of-consciousness: 'The concrete episodes swim in my memory like small islands: that is the structure of the story'.

It is in *Interview with Myself* that Wolf first uses the term 'authentic' – to denote not objective factual reality, but subjective experience, a category of 'truth' verifiable through the author's creative imagination. The 'authentic' presence of the author (in the form of narrator) is the precondition for the new definition Christa Wolf gives of the concept of 'realism'. In her subsequent conversation with East German literary critic Hans Kaufmann, she uses the term 'inner' or 'subjective' authenticity, to define the central role of experience for modern prose. A further innovative idea, first tried out against imaginary critics in *Interview with Myself* and revolutionary at the time *Christa T.* was written, is Wolf's insistence that 'private, sometimes profoundly inner conflicts' are a subject worthy of literary treatment. As society becomes more differentiated, the need arises for a more probing mode of writing which takes account of the psychological fabric of its individual members.

Wolf warns her contemporaries not to lose sight of their high aims of spiritual renewal and self-realisation. To this end she quotes from the diary of fellow writer and veteran socialist Johannes R. Becher, with whom she shares the utopian concept of hope: 'For this profound unrest of the human soul is nothing but the premonition and the ability to sense that man has not yet come to himself. This coming-to-oneself: what is it?' (From J.R. Becher, *Auf andere Art so grosse Hoffnung. Tagebuch 1950/In a Different Way, Such High Hope, Diary 1950* [1969]). At this stage Wolf, in her belief that society may move nearer to reaching this goal by being aware of the needs of its individual members, is more optimistic than Becher. In adopting this new attitude to prose, Wolf created a breach with the prescribed official method of writing, and fell foul of the strict ruling against 'formalist' or experimental methods of literary production which had led to the censorship of all 'modernist' writing, German and foreign, in the GDR of the 1950s and early 1960s. In the wake of the Czech Kafka Conference of 1963, a serious confrontation between writers and critics took place over prescriptive official attitudes at the Writers' Congress of 1965: attitudes which had negative repercussions on Wolf's political career and on her official position as a writer.

In 1965, Christa Wolf wrote a short story, *Juninachmittag* (*June Afternoon*, published in 1967 and since reprinted in numerous anthologies of GDR prose, though not to my knowledge translated into English), which fulfilled in every respect the criteria of modern prose which were to be laid down later in *The Reader and the Writer*. This short text not only constitutes a radical change in Wolf's own style and approach to writing, it is also rightly considered by many critics as the beginning of an altogether new approach to narrative prose in the GDR, an approach which has since been adopted by most serious writers.

Christa Wolf begins with an address to her readers in which she dispels the illusion that they are about to hear a proper story with a plot, a chronological, third-person narrative, and an idea or moral to take away and make use of, to learn from. Instead, she offers to those readers who possess the right kind of imagination a 'vision', a kind of 'dream'. By involving the reader in the narrative process, Wolf appeals to the critical faculties of reflection and self-reflection. *June Afternoon* is written largely in the form of interior monologue and reported speech from the perspective of an 'I' – the narrator – who does not disguise her identity as the author. The setting is a garden suburb of Berlin close to the border dividing East and West, recognizable as Kleinmachnow where Wolf and her family lived when the story was written. The main characters correspond to Wolf's own family. Others – neighbours – appear at the periphery and intrude only briefly into the life of the family. The setting, a luscious garden, is interpreted by some critics as symbolic of the fertile and free-ranging imagination of the writer. Yet limitations are imposed on the narrator's imagination: during the afternoon spent in the garden she does not move from her place in a deck chair. From here she receives a range of outside influences to which she adds her reactions, reflections, memories and emotions: joy, happiness, anxiety and fear. The afternoon culminates in her withdrawing from this environment for a short period of intense introspection, when she becomes aware of how close to death we are in life. This realization releases a new strength, a determination to rid herself of all superfluous burdens, to be free for the essential tasks. It is not difficult, with hindsight, to interpret the narrator's burden as the doctrines and prescriptive practices which Wolf had absorbed in her early years as a writer and critic, and even as a student of German literature. But despite her introspection, the narrator remains firmly bound to reality, to the garden, to her family who operate through tightly interwoven relationships, to the neighbours and their obsessions and idiosyncrasies: she is also acutely aware of the political reality of the Cold War. Against all this, the narrator evokes language and imagination as restraining and regenerating impulses.

June Afternoon, as a piece of 'experimental' prose, contains most of the narrative elements which were to be developed in a more complex and comprehensive narrative fabric in *The Quest for Christa T.* Once again, Wolf avoids the restrictions of a linear plot and two-dimensional characters by introducing the subjective perspective of a first-person narrator who has strong links with the author. In a preface, the narrator explains to her prospective readers the reason for her writing and her intended approach. The premature death of a friend (Christa T. was in fact a fellow student of the Wolfs' who had died of leukemia) is taken as a challenge: the quest is to find out more about the true character of a person who had not fitted the role assigned to her by society. Memory is put to work, not through simple recall, but through a reworking of the past, to recreate the process of living and thus to understand Christa T.'s real significance within her own time and beyond it. In this way, the author adds to her subject the dimension of 'depth', of 'subjective authenticity', by having recourse to her own experience.

In defiance of established Socialist Realist doctrines, the narrator challenges the notion that she must conceive her character as an example for others to follow. Instead, Christa T. seems to follow the impulses coming from a person as she lived, a person who involves the narrator in a process of reflecting once more on the past. Three years after Christa T.'s death in 1963, the time is ripe for the narrator to look back over her friend's life, from the moment of their first meeting as sixteen-year-old schoolgirls in 1944, as the Third Reich was drawing to its end, to the final stages of her fatal illness and her death. For long stretches, Christa T.'s life resembles that of the narrator and is representative of the lives of many young people of Wolf's generation who grew up first under National Socialism and then under socialism. Yet, in some essential respects Christa T. differs from the narrator and her peers. This is first captured in the image of the sixteen-year-old Christa T. simulating a trumpet call, with this gesture defiantly asserting her individuality. Her background is different, too: the daughter of a forester, she has experienced class discrimination, but defies this form of exclusion by playing only with boys. At school, she asserts her will by withholding approval of a teacher who proclaims ardent National Socialist views. Thus she earns the respect and admiration of the narrator, who now realizes that it is possible to be different, to avoid conformity.

The withholding of approval, as opposed to actual dissent, remains characteristic of this figure: it sets her apart from her contemporaries during the early postwar years in the GDR. Like Christa Wolf, Christa T. experiences uprooting from her home town (readily recognizable as Landsberg). Her deepest crisis, reflecting the rift between child and adult, occurs when she discovers the body of a frozen infant in the snow. Affinity to children, and an intense abhorrence of violence (the killing of a cat, the mutilation of a frog by one of her pupils, cause her depression and despair) are early indications of a sensitivity which make her unfit for the world in which she grows up.

In retrospect, the narrator casts a critical light on the 1950s – the years when she and Christa T. were students – as a time when the individual was not given the right to be different, and the general tenor was one of adapting to a fast moving technological world. Christa T. nevertheless remains true to herself, though at the cost of deep self-doubt: she even contemplates suicide. As a young teacher Christa T. tries hard to uphold her ideal that each individual is worthy of respect and self-respect, only to be defeated by a young generation of pupils who are prepared to renounce their individuality and conform to set standards. 'Adaptation is the nucleus of health', she is told by a former pupil who accuses her of placing too much emphasis on imagination. For the rest of her life, as wife to a country vet and the mother of two children, Christa T. puts all her energies into pursuing her aim: not to adapt for the sake of conformity, but to remain alive, sensitive and capable of changing. Not to stagnate, but to extend the limits of oneself and experiment with life: this is Christa T.'s legacy which the narrator wants to uphold.

Christa T.'s death should not be seen as a negative ending, even if critics have sometimes concentrated on this apparently pessimistic, defeatist aspect of the book. Wolf's own intention, clearly stated in her *Interview with Myself*, was to remember Christa T.'s life in such a way that it could be seen as complete in itself, cut short only by the lack of time to explore other, fuller possibilities. The narrator makes it her task to show the fullness of the life of an individual who was out of step with her time, only because her time lacked the vision she possessed. The motto of the book: 'This coming-to-oneself: what is it?' is demonstrated through one individual who looks ahead, and at the same time seeks within herself for answers to this question. If Christa T. failed herself and others, it was in her diffidence in expressing herself through creative writing. Only in this respect does her life remain fragmentary in the eyes of the narrator, who sees the deepest reason for Christa T.'s failure to find her true vocation in her difficulty in saying 'I'. To be at one with herself, to admit to her true identity is but a 'hope', a utopian ideal, for Christa T. In writing about her, the author establishes the identity of her character, and through her finds her own identity.

It is hardly surprising that *The Quest for Christa T.* caused confusion among the cultural authorities and was heavily condemned by those who adhered to doctrinal Socialist Realism. Others, particularly Western critics, read the book as a testimonial of dissidence. This worked to the author's disadvantage, so that a first – limited – edition of 1967 was withdrawn and the book did not come out until the following year. As with all Wolf's books, the response of readers indicated she had touched a nerve.

One subject which presented special problems to writers in the GDR was the treatment of the relation between the fascist past and the socialist present, both as individual experience and as literary subject. As Wolf points out in conversation with Hans Kaufmann, the GDR had been premature in declaring the fascist past 'overcome' through anti-fascist re-education after the war or through the example set by writers who had had firsthand experience of anti-fascist resistance whilst living in exile. Consequently, the literary treatment of the subject either produced model anti-fascist heroes, or, in the work of writers of the 1950s, models of re-education through raising class consciousness in the young by veteran socialists. In *The Quest for Christa T.*, Christa Wolf had already cast doubt on the effectiveness of such examples. In the 1960s and 1970s, other writers, notably Führmann, Bobrowski, Kant and Anna Seghers, began to reopen the subject. But it was left to Christa Wolf to face up to the conflicts of a generation of Germans who had absorbed the new socialism without having gained insight into the deeper effects of National Socialism, and to lift the veil that had been drawn over the memory. One reason, no doubt, was Wolf's burning interest in the psychological depth of human nature: another was her quest to understand the reasons for the inhibitions she had experienced in her own development as a writer. The result was her most complex narrative prose work *Kindheitsmuster* (*A Model Childhood*, or more accurately, *Patterns of Childhood*) of 1976. But this subject had preoccupied Wolf since the late 1960s at least, and had been treated tentatively in several shorter prose sketches.

'Christa T.' is mentioned briefly as a school friend of the narrator in *A Model Childhood*, one of many indications that both works belong in the same context of Christa Wolf's development. Both works are concerned with the search for self, and both look back over a period of time. But the gap between narrative past – the author's childhood – and narrative present is considerably widened, so that the problems of how to write have increased. The author takes the unusual step (following Virginia Woolf's example, it has been suggested) of making the problem of writing transparent in the narration itself. The constant transition from narrative prose to essay style is an integral part of the book and adds the dimension of 'subjective authenticity'. But the subject matter itself, the author's personal experience, also demands a degree of authenticity.

The narrative operates on three levels, which are joined together in the narrator's consciousness. First (though not the starting point of the book) is the historical level, the childhood and early adolescence, covering the years 1933 to 1947, of the character Nelly Jordan, who represents the narrator's own youth. The second level consists of a short journey in July 1971 by the narrator and her family – husband, brother and daughter Lenka – back to the town, now in Poland, where Nelly Jordan grew up and which she left in January 1945. This forms the link between the narrative past and present, and acts as yardstick for the narrator's memories. The third level is concurrent with the period of writing (1972 to 1975), and creates the strongest impression of identity between narrator and author. Although all three levels proceed chronologically, they are tightly interwoven – often in mid-sentence – reflecting once again an associative, stream-of-consciousness mode of narration. A central narrative problem standing between author and subject is the use of narrative viewpoint, the question whether to write in the first or the third person. The solution is found in a compromise: the narrator writes about her childhood in the third person; while for the other two levels – which relate to both past and present – she uses the second person singular 'thou'. As Wolf indicates in the *Discussion on a Model Childhood*, she envisages the ending as a coming together of the third and the second person in the first person 'I'. This does indeed take place on the last page of the book, where the narrator reflects on what has been achieved in the process of analysing the child within herself, but she leaves unanswered the question of whether she has found her identity through evoking the child; has the child merely retreated yet further from investigation?

Two major themes of the book, however, are given substantial exposure: one is the question of memory in its various functions, in particular the ability to hide and suppress what is uncomfortable; the other is the evocation of the mentality and milieu of an average lower-middle-class family who live the double standards and half truths attendant on their uneasy truce with National Socialism. What emerges, mainly through the figure of Nelly, who participates eagerly in the Hitler Youth movement and initially finds little cause to question her own motives, are the unconscious strategies of self-deception and insincerity arising from a fear of being different. Wolf not only probes her memory, but also tests her sincerity and openness towards the present. In this respect, the fifteen-year-old daughter Lenka has an important role, not only in challenging the mother's (the narrator's) ability to convey past experience, but also in demonstrating a different attitude towards truthfulness. Lenka reacts spontaneously and unselfconsciously against violence and the abuse of power (in Chile, in Vietnam), and accuses her mother of using 'pseudo-language'. In Lenka, Wolf creates an ideal character, free of fear and self-deception, whom she sets in a sharp contrast to the Nelly figure.

Wolf admits that her concern in writing about her own childhood was not to ask what led to National Socialism, but to analyse the influence of the past on present-day attitudes. This is summed up in the question: 'How have we become the way we are?' Her major concern is to uncover a potentially dangerous political compromise made for the sake of material security, and to warn about deference to authority, since both lead to war. When A Model Childhood was published in late 1976, Wolf had already entered a new phase in her self-understanding as a writer within her own society. Influenced also by the repercussions of Wolf Biermann's exile in November 1976, she turned her attention fully to two subjects which had begun to preoccupy her at least from the time The Quest for Christa T. was written: the period of early Romanticism in Germany, and the place women have been given (or denied) in society since then. In retrospective assessment of this stage in her writing, during a conversation with Frauke Meyer-Gosau in 1982, Wolf stresses her interest in the 'outsiders' who lived during the period broadly between the French Revolution and the Restoration in Germany. 'Outsider' status was assigned to both women and intellectuals (or more precisely, to producers of art). This she sees as part of a larger process of alienation and self-alienation in industrial society, set in train by advances in technology and natural sciences and reflected in the division between the rational and the irrational, between politics and art.

Two female literary figures move to the centre of Wolf's work of the late 1970s: Karoline von Günderode (1780–1806), eldest daughter of an impoverished aristocratic family who from the secluded life of a ladies' convent had formed ties with several members of the early Romantic circle in and around Heidelberg at the beginning of the nineteenth century. Among these was Bettina Brentano (1785–1859), sister of the poet Clemens and later wife of another poet Achim von Arnim, whose life as a Prussian landowner she shared faithfully until his death, though it imposed considerable constraints on her own creative spirit.

The friendship between the two women – invested with fervour on Bettine's side, with restraint on Günderrode's (these are Christa Wolf's spellings of the women's names) – left its traces in an exchange of letters on which Bettine later based her epistolary novel Die Günderode (1839). Günderrode has been virtually ignored by literary historians – including the Marxist Georg Lukács, who excluded her from the literary canon along with other 'outsider' figures of the early nineteenth century:

Büchner, Kleist and Hölderlin. These omissions evoked protest from Anna Seghers in her famous correspondence with Lukács in exile in 1938–9. Taking sides with Seghers, Wolf resurrects these figures in her prose and essay work, defending them against the overpowering influence of a classical age. Bettine, in literary history, has been cast in the role of an emotional, subjective, unreliable chronicler of the revered Goethe: on her first epistolary novel *Goethes Briefwechsel mit einem Kinde* (1835) (*Goethe's Correspondence with a Child*) her literary reputation rested for almost a century.

Christa Wolf casts fresh light on the two women and their relationship with each other, with the small avantgardist circle of early Romantics, and with society at large in two substantial essays and one fictional prose work written between 1977 and 1979: these include the novella *Kein Ort. Nirgends* (*No Place on Earth*), and an essay on Günderrode (1978), entitled 'Der Schatten eines Traumes. Ein Entwurf' ('The Shadow of a Dream. A Sketch') which formed the foreword to a new selection by Wolf from Günderrode's poetic and epistolary work. This book was published in the GDR in 1979 under the same title – *The Shadow of a Dream*, a quotation from one of Günderrode's letters.

In Wolf's reading, Günderrode's life is restricted to a mere shadow, a dream of the life in which she so eagerly wished to participate. As a woman, she could find self-realization only through writing: under an assumed (male) name, Tian, she published poetry, plays and prose and, as was the custom at the time, wrote many letters. Not only because of her position as an impoverished aristocrat but also through her irrepressible need to write, Günderrode was pushed to the very margins of society. Wolf sees here the cause of the insoluble conflict of Günderrode's life, which drove her to suicide in 1806 (near Winkel on the Rhine, Wolf's setting for *No Place on Earth*). This was not her unhappy relationship with a married man – the philosopher Creuzer – but rather the unattainably high standards she set for herself, her aim being to reach perfection both in love and in writing. Her adherence to the aesthetic rules dictated by the classical cannon under Goethe's reign caused deep conflict with her own inner visions and images. Günderrode's situation is in many ways close to that of Wolf's earlier literary figure Christa T., and also a reflection of Wolf's own antagonistic position in her search for self. It is the essential contrast to this position which attracts Wolf to Bettine von Arnim, about whom in 1979 she wrote a comprehensive essay as an introduction to a new East German edition of Bettine's novel *Die Günderode* (Insel, Leipzig 1981). Wolf's title: 'Nun ja! Das nächste Leben geht aber heute an' ('Yes, Indeed. But the Next Life Begins Today') is taken from Bettine's letters. Wolf adds the subtitle: 'A Letter about Bettine', and addresses it to a woman friend, another writer, in the hope of evoking a sense of kinship with Bettine as their 'precursor'.

In choosing the letter form Wolf not only distances herself from the established mode of literary criticism but also expresses an affinity with Bettine's choice of the letter as the only authentic way of writing about an emotional, highly subjective and sensitive subject, the friendship between two young women. This, for Bettine, was conceived as a form of 'platonic' love, because of its inseparable expression of feeling and thinking; and for Wolf this embodies poetic spirit lost in our own time:

> Shall I deny that I feel some envy and sadness when I read and imagine how, in all innocence, two young women, Germans, relate to each other; for the poetic spirit, the mark of true humanity thrives only with the innocent. Those women had the poetic spirit; we have poetry, but poetic relationships are denied to us.

Wolf appeals to a need which she detects in her friend (and in herself) to overcome the enforced and self-imposed separation of body and mind, so freeing language from the restrictions of a one-sided rationality. This is expressed in feminist terms:

> I appeal to your passionate attempts to remove, with the help of unbound language, layers of unlived life which separate your mind, your consciousness, your emotions, your body from itself.

For Wolf, the two women represent a dichotomy which she herself experiences: Günderrode, with her high standards, never achieved any influence in her own society, while Bettine, not opting for perfection, involved herself actively and passionately in the political issues of the period between 1832 and 1840 – she dedicated her *Günderode* book to the students, and another to the King of Prussia.

In her novella *No Place on Earth* (1979) Wolf 'invents' a chance encounter between Karoline von Günderrode and Heinrich von Kleist (1777–1811) at the village of Winkel on the Rhine, on another June afternoon, this one in 1804. The setting is a tea party in the house of a wealthy businessman and patron of the arts, Merten, who gathers around him a number of figures from the literary and political scene of the day, among them the Romantic poet Brentano and the Prussian statesman Savigny. The publication of Karoline's first volume of poems (albeit under an assumed name) makes her for the moment the centre of attention. Kleist arouses interest, too: an unexpected guest, he has just come through a period of the deepest self-doubt, having been dismissed from the Napoleonic army and having destroyed his fragmentary play *Robert Guiscard*. Feeling misunderstood and misjudged by the company (who represent society in the wider sense), Günderrode and Kleist discover a deep affinity with one another. They read each others' innermost thoughts and Karoline is able to interpret them. She recognizes their common need to reach beyond rigidly defined gender roles: but where Kleist bemoans these as naturally given – 'Sometimes I find it unendurable that nature has split the human being into man and woman' – Karoline points more precisely to the psychological nature of the conflict: 'What you mean is that man and woman have a hostile relationship inside you. As they do in me.' For a moment, in a spirit of mutual recognition and acceptance of their 'otherness', they rise above alienating role concepts.

By choosing to bring together two figures whose real lives ended in suicide, Wolf stresses that time and circumstance allowed neither to achieve self-realization by overcoming a deep sense of alienation from themselves and from their time. Wolf here takes up a theme already struck in *The Quest for Christa T.*, but now in a darker and more pessimistic vein. Whereas in the earlier work the narrator had transported the memory of her character into a time which was open towards individuality, for people like Kleist and Günderrode there is 'no place on earth', 'no hope'. In a tone of dark foreboding, Wolf sees herself cast in the role of their successor, forced into a position of speaking against her better judgement:

> The wicked spoor left in time's wake as it flees us. You precursors, feet bleeding.... And we, still greedy for the ashen taste of words. Not yet mute as is suitable.

No Place on Earth can be read on two levels: it conveys a vivid and intimate impression of the cultural and social climate of the early nineteenth century, and it suggests parallels with the isolation and frustration among the more discerning intellectuals of the late 1970s. As Wolf points out in her interviews of the early 1980s, this experience not only reflects a specific situation – the after-effects of the Biermann protest – but a much more general sense of impotence among writers vis-à-vis those political strategies which have led to a worldwide nuclear arms race. This is how Wolf, at the end of the 'Günderrode' essay, outlines the situation of her own time:

> The rigorous division of labour reaps its harvest. The producers of material and those of spiritual values face each other as strangers from different shores, prevented from generating conditions which would enable them to live together. They all are exposed to the destruction, not always apparent. Poets, that is no lament, are predestined to be victims and self victims.

If *No Place on Earth* marks the lowest point in Wolf's assessment of humanity's chances of overcoming self-alienation, this has not led her to a fatalistic acceptance of the inevitable. The experiences of the late 1970s, though deeply distressing, may even have had the salutary effect of making her more reliant on her resources as a writer and – increasingly – as a woman. From the early 1980s, feminist perspectives come more forcefully to the fore in Wolf's writing as she becomes more open towards women's movements in the West. In her contribution to the Berlin Peace Meeting of December 1981, she argued that the exclusion of women from culture and civilization throughout the history of the West is the cause of man's fatal tendency to self-destruction in the present. She looks for the beginning of this development in the mythological past, and locates it at the moment of the Trojan wars, of which only heroic (male) records survive. Wolf now began to research the myth from a fresh perspective, making the figure of Cassandra her central point of reference. In the traditional rendering, Cassandra – daughter of the Trojan king Priam and his queen Hecuba – receives her gift as seer and prophet from the God Apollo, and warns of Troy's fall should it enter into war with the Greeks. But her prophecy goes unheeded, and after ten years of battle Troy falls to the Greeks, Priam and Hecuba having lost all their sons and daughters.

In Wolf's story *Cassandra* (1983) we meet the prophetess at the gates of Mycenae: she is the prisoner of Agamemnon, the Greek leader who conquered Troy where Achilles has failed, and is now about to be executed by Agamemnon's wife Clytemnestra. Mounted on a chariot, Cassandra brings to memory the contradictory processes of her people's destruction and self-annihilation on the one hand and her own self-realization on the other. Only the first few lines are spoken by the narrator/author, establishing her bond with the literary figure, after which the 'I' merges with the voice of Cassandra in the ominous line: 'Keeping in step with the story, I make my way into death'. From this point onwards, Wolf follows the dictate of her central figure, recording Cassandra's inner voice, memories, dreams, reflections. This voice has a strong rhythm, in contrast with the darker, more melodic language of *No Place on Earth*. Only in the last lines does Cassandra's voice fade, as the narrator takes up the thread again with the words: 'Here is the place. These stone lions looked at her. They seem to move in the shifting light'.

Wolf refuses to regard her sources – Homer's *Iliad* and Aeschylus's *Oresteia* – as reliable authorities. Against these she pits her own interpretation of Cassandra, making her an embodiment of the non-heroic, subjective and subversive aspects of war, an embodiment of everything suppressed by the heroic epics. Their fatalistic trend is transformed by Cassandra's interpretation of her own fate and that of her people. She cannot prevent their self-destruction, but she can save herself and a few like-minded friends from becoming mere objects in this process.

It is not Wolf's intention, however, to replace the ancient myth with a modern one, but to make as thorough a study as possible of the social and psychological dimensions of her subject, and in so doing once again to establish links between past and present: 'My interest in the Cassandra figure: to retrace the path out of the myth, into its (supposed) social and historical coordinates'. Cassandra's role as priestess and seer is therefore not primarily a gift from the gods, but something she has chosen for herself as the only alternative open to her as a woman who would otherwise become an object of men's desire and will – as is demonstrated by the fate of her sister Polyxena. But her office alienates Cassandra from herself, since it binds her in duty and loyalty to her father as the king, who in turn becomes more and more the object of war preparations. Cassandra 'sees' through the lies and propaganda devices mobilised to bring about a war which has become inevitable for economic reasons, and not – as the myth would have it – for the sake of the beautiful Helen. But Cassandra's voice remains powerless, as a woman she cannot influence events. This leaves her with the task of recording her deep horror at the senseless slaughter of Greek and Trojan men alike, among them her beloved brothers. She brings to light the fear and agony of violent death, deflating the notion of 'heroism'. The Greek Achilles, the immaculate hero of the myth, becomes the epitome of inhuman behaviour: Cassandra speaks of him only with the epithet 'the brute'. Out of weakness, he kills and rapes both her brother and Penthesilea, the Amazon leader who joins forces with the Trojans. Wolf here rejects the option of women adopting male role models by showing that it leads to self-alienation and self-destruction. She equally rejects the orgiastic dances of women, Amazons and Trojans, to celebrate, ritualize and avenge the death of Penthesilea: she calls these 'a procession leading nowhere on earth: leading to madness' and to more killing.

Cassandra's true voice makes itself heard in a state of being 'beyond herself', in an articulate cry interpreted by those who hold power in Troy as madness. But this cry of the soul reveals her deepest needs as a human being. It is only when she is physically removed from the Trojans through imprisonment that her gift of seeing reveals itself in its true nature: as a vision of her self, her need for a free exchange of love and human understanding. This she finds, albeit temporarily, in the community of people – women, children and a few men – who live outside the patriarchal social confines of the Trojan citadel at the foot of mount Ida, close to nature, worshipping Cybele, the goddess of the irrational, and creating an oasis of peace and humanity. Here Cassandra is allowed to be herself, to love and to express her emotions through body and soul, free of fear and the need to adapt to alien standards. Here she recovers her subjectivity and her trust in human beings. She remains faithful to herself to the end, when she rejects the offer to escape death with Aeneas, the only Trojan man she could love, because he accepts her as she is. But she refuses to be part of an inevitable involvement with the 'heroic' deeds which lie in store for

Aeneas. Instead, she takes with her to her death the knowledge that a community of peaceful individuals exists, hoping before her death to pass this knowledge on to one of Clytemnestra's female servants, who will in turn tell it to her own daughter, thus creating a small stream of female oral tradition which might surive alongside the strong male current of the heroic epics.

In the four lectures which precede the story, Wolf shares with her readers the search for Cassandra with the question: 'Who was Cassandra before people wrote about her?' She is motivated in her search by a desire to free the literary figure from its deformation by male aesthetics: 'For she is a creation of the poets, she speaks only through them, we have only their view of her'. In her preface to the lectures, Wolf rejects the notion of herself offering formal aesthetic criteria to her listeners, arguing that 'poetics' are a patriarchal concept. Instead, she proceeds to pursue the 'female' ways of writing which she has already discovered in the work of women of the Romantic era. Consequently, Wolf now experiments with a range of non-literary forms: her four lectures consist of travelogue, diary and letter. Separating her reflections on writing from the narrative proper is a move away from her previous habit of merging essay and prose.

In the first two lectures – headed 'Travel Report' – she considers her gradual acquaintance with the figure of Cassandra through the environment, the Greek mainland and the islands, the ancient palaces of Mycenae and Knossos, in her travels with her husband in the Easter of 1980. During this time she read the classical sources – Homer, Aeschylus, Euripides – and discovered their deformation and suppression of women. She opens her mind to traces of a matriarchal, peaceful Minoan culture which preceded the patriarchal societies of Ancient Greece, which in their turn led Troy to sever its last links with the matriarchal past.

The third lecture is subtitled 'Work Diary' and dated May 1980. It was written at the Wolfs' country retreat at Meteln in Mecklenburg, and contains, among further thoughts about Cassandra, a detailed account of a discussion with visiting friends about the chances of surviving a nuclear war and the options open to writers to counter the tendency towards self-destruction. Here Wolf declares her support for unilateral nuclear disarmament in a passage which, in the GDR edition, fell to the censors because it conflicted with the then prevailing official line of armed peace. Wolf also refers to the dangers of deformation of myths through propaganda, citing as her authority the correspondence between Thomas Mann and the Hungarian philosopher Karl Kerényi in 1934.

The fourth lecture is written in the form of a letter addressed to A. – a friend with a background similar to Wolf's own – once again from the Mecklenburg retreat. Wolf here openly declares herself on the side of women as she pursues the history of their suppression in myths and literature, although she refuses to be drawn into any notion of feminist writing:

> I will not yield to the urge to talk about 'the position of women', to cite observations, to quote from letters. One day, no doubt, I must do so, if only to give legitimacy to what women write about women.

The focus of the lecture is Ingeborg Bachmann, to whom Wolf had been drawn since writing *Christa T.*, and in whose footsteps she followed when delivering her Frankfurt lectures. In interpreting Bachmann's poem *Explain to me, Love,* Wolf disregards prescribed aesthetic rules in uncovering the voice of the female 'I' crying out against the alienating influence of thinking. She brings to light the ambiguities without trying to rationalise them. Her questions remain unanswered, just as the poem itself consists of unanswerable questions culminating in the lines: 'Must someone think? Isn't he missed?' The question begs the answer: through pure rationality a woman's selfhood, her need for love, her instincts, her joy, are suppressed as she becomes 'objective'. The causes for the suppression of women's voices are to be sought in a prevailing system of aesthetics, reinforced in German Classicism by the 'great' writers, notably Goethe, whom she once again – and more severely than in either the *Günderrode* or in the *Bettine* essays – takes to task.

Wolf's criticism, levelled at Goethe's concept of the classical Greek age from which he derived his own aesthetic principles, is that he refers to the patriarchal age after the first Olympiad in 776 BC, thereby suppressing an earlier mythical age of a matriarchal culture. Through her reading of *Faust Part 2*, Wolf demonstrates that Goethe knew and feared the dark, subconscious, mythical forces, and that this is apparent in his mission to descend to the subterranean realm of the 'Mothers'; and also in the witchcraft and magic of the classical *Walpurgisnacht*. Wolf sees a direct correlation between the suppression of the subconscious, the mythical and matriarchal, and the conscious, rational, self-denying adherence to firmly established aesthetic rules. She states more clearly than ever before that she no longer wishes to accept a canon of prescribed aesthetics and an 'authority of literary genres'. Through her discourses with women, either as mythical or literary figures, or as women writers to whom she feels a particular affinity – Ingeborg Bachmann, Marie-Luise Fleisser and Virginia Woolf – Christa Wolf has developed a different perspective, a change of heart as fundamental as the change brought about by her first encounter with Marxism:

> With the widening of my visual angle and the readjustment of my depth of focus, my viewing lens (through which I perceive our time, all of us, you,

myself) has undergone a decisive change. It is comparable to that decisive change that occurred more than thirty years ago, when I first became acquainted with Marxist theory and attitudes, a liberating and illuminating experience which altered my thinking, my view, what I felt about and demanded of myself.

Whilst *Cassandra* received a very positive reception in the West, critics in the GDR have reacted with some scepticism to this work, in particular to Wolf's treatment of women's issues and her stance on unarmed peace. (The GDR edition appeared almost a year after the West German edition, and with some passages removed.) Once again, the reaction of readers is quite different: young people especially find in this work an acceptable alternative to official debates on peace and emancipation. In the West, Cassandra has become a cult figure.

In her latest book *Störfall* (*Accident,* 1986), Christa Wolf addresses herself to issues which have by necessity become common concerns of everyone living in Europe: the direct consequences of Chernobyl for the individual, for society and for the future of humanity. The book is conceived and written in the form of a diary, and the narrator is again clearly identifiable as the author. She goes through successive stages of anxiety in the course of one day as she receives media reports of the fallout a few days after the disaster. At the same time, she is trying to contain her fears about her brother who is undergoing an operation to remove a brain tumour. The operation will determine not just whether he lives or dies, but also whether, if he lives, he can continue to put his rational faculties to use as a scientist.

The narrator is alone, separated from her family in a country retreat in Mecklenburg. She records faithfully, in complete detail and with no apparent attempt at creative ordering, the negative stimuli she receives from outside (the news) and within herself (her emotions as she imagines her brother on the operating table). As in the earlier works, a tension is created which leads to introspection and brings the narrator to the brink of despair. But she regains her equilibrium as she performs simple, ordinary daily activities – gardening, cooking, shopping, meeting neighbours and listening to their mundane problems. She keeps in touch with her family and a friend through telephone conversations and through them is helped to regain a sense of perspective. Wolf's latest short prose work obviously has much in common with *June Afternoon*, written more than twenty years earlier: its concern in particular with the question of survival, as a thinking and feeling individual, in the present age. The writer again speaks directly to her readers and shares with them her sense of isolation and impotence vis-à-vis dominant political strategies.

Christa Wolf has been taken to task, particularly in the West German press, for an apparent disregard of literary form in her latest story, and for giving a serious subject such apparently mundane treatment. But given her position on aesthetic rules and her determination to allow the 'female voice' to be heard, Wolf remains consistent and true to herself. She has moved a long way: from a writer primarily concerned with a utopian vision of a socialist humanity to one who puts before herself and her readers the choice of remaining a subject and alive, as against becoming mere objects of political, scientific and economic power structures.

Department of German
University of Edinburgh
May 1988

1

THE FOURTH DIMENSION

A Conversation with Joachim Walther*

Joachim Walther: *To begin with I'd like to ask you a few questions about extrinsic things. What kind of working conditions do you need in order to write?*

External conditions are not immensely important to me, though I do have a few essential requirements. I need familiar surroundings, because I find it difficult to concentrate and an unfamiliar environment distracts me. When I'm travelling, for example, I will make notes but not write. Another important condition is to get a reasonable amount of sleep, which is often a problem, especially in periods when I am writing intensively. To this I could add the need for a relatively regular daily routine. I like to begin as early as possible, be able to work for four hours before lunch with a minimum of interruptions, then a bit more in the afternoon, maybe two or three hours if I can manage it. And not too many distractions. But I'm not particularly dependent on moods or stimulation – nothing out of the ordinary in other words.

Joachim Walther: *Do you make a point of writing regularly, do you set yourself a daily target?*

Regularly, yes, that's absolutely essential. As far as I'm concerned, a day on which I don't write is basically lost. But I don't set myself a definite target. I have learned with time that I can't keep to it, and continuing to set yourself goals you can't achieve over a long period of time leads to nothing but dissatisfaction with yourself. Ideally, of course, one would write a page a day. But it would be impossible to keep that kind of pace

*Originally published in J. Walther, *Meinetwegen Schmetterlinge* (Berlin 1973).

1

up. It would mean writing a whole novel in a year: that's ridiculous. There are times when you can work at that pace .... But one ought to work every day, certainly.

Joachim Walther: *What characteristics must a writer possess?*

That is something one cannot generalize about. The hidden motive behind your question is probably the hope that the person you ask will come out with the characteristics they see themselves as having. Let's say, in terms of basic characteristics (which are necessary to other professions, too) you have to be tenacious, not governed by moods, hard-working and thorough. In addition, you need to have a very strong, perpetually self-rejuvenating, unflagging interest in people, social relations and developments within society. A great deal of curiosity. Keen sensitivity. And a relatively low pain threshold. Of course being highly sensitive and at the same time having a low pain threshold causes a lot of discomfort. I know people who are sensitive only in relation to themselves. It seems to me it would be ideal if writers were sensitive to other people's experiences as if they were their own, and to their own almost as if they were a stranger's. We must include amongst these 'characteristics' a certain inner freedom – at this point, though, it becomes obvious that talking about 'characteristics' isn't going to get us very far. We should really be talking about behavioural qualities, which are based on specific social processes and are therefore not immutable. Ruthlessness, for example, which I would demand, can only be conceived of as productive behaviour in productive societies, otherwise it becomes destructive ... then art is not possible, because this has to make things into objects, i.e. ruthlessly distance things that one has previously been intimately involved with.

Joachim Walther: *We are left with a dilemma: let us suppose that, being sensitive to the suffering of others, you see someone whose suffering you could alleviate on a practical level, if you stopped writing for a time. But, if you did help this person, then others would appear who were suffering just as much and therefore equally in need of help. You would be in danger of becoming a samaritan and giving up writing for 'action'.*

Yes, this is the age-old contradiction between living and writing, between observation and action. When you are faced with a dilemma of this kind, then only praxis will show which of the possible ways out has the stronger pull on you. I know the problem well. Whenever I've been in a position to help someone directly, I've always felt a need, almost a compulsion, to go and do so. And I do go and help. On the other hand, the question is whether the urge to write is so strong that it asserts itself over all distractions. It is a difficult balancing act. Now and then it happens that my relationships with people temporarily lay more claim to me than my writing. But writing has for some time been my most important and constant motivation.

Joachim Walther: *Do you think that writing can compensate for life? Cocteau once said that the male artist has no need of women since in the creative process he unites the feminine and the masculine.*

I have noticed that male writers show 'feminine' (in the original sense of the word) traces and female writers 'masculine' ones. But that isn't what you mean. I have a very strong need for human relationships and writing cannot be a substitute for them. Sometimes I get taken over too much by this need for people. I'm highly inquisitive about people and constantly need to make new acquaintances or keep old ones going. I see relationships with others, in all possible forms – love, friendship, comradeship, co-operation at work – as one of the problems of life. But I don't confuse life and writing, or see life as my 'material'. If I'm with somebody it never occurs to me that they could be a character: I never think, there's an interesting situation, I could use it somewhere. That would be blasphemous.... No, writing isn't life itself, but something derived from it, in the first instance anyway. Writing is the processing of experience, not a substitute for it. That which is written can, though, due to the special role of our second signalling system, become a primary experience.

Joachim Walther: *Are you able to trace ideas back and locate their origins?*

Sometimes I can. Sometimes I can remember the exact moment, and even the physical circumstances, in which I worked out what I wanted to say. I often forget it though, too, and am later surprised to come across a note of it. It seems to me that a basic precondition for such ideas to emerge is an inner restlessness, an accumulated restlessness which is at first diffuse and undirected. It's not just a case of sitting around and waiting to be struck by an idea. You are constantly doing something or other. In the midst of all this activity all the diffuse strands of this restlessness somehow (one never knows quite how) converge on a focal point and the idea is 'born'. It is one of the most beautiful moments. Recently, just before I woke up from a dream, I was saying out loud an idea for a chapter I was working on. When I woke up, I could still remember what it was I'd said and I still liked it.

Joachim Walther: *Do you think an idea can be consciously induced, in the sense that as one gathers one's observations and carries out one's studies, one is enriching something within oneself and waiting – not inactively, but nonetheless waiting – to make the leap?*

That's a different kind of idea. What I was talking about was an idea about something of which you have no inkling at all beforehand, a story-line, for instance. But even at a later stage, you have to rely on new ideas coming to your aid, that's what's so terrible. Supposing I know what I want to write about; the subject matter is there, so I can make a start. I begin collecting material. I make a lot of notes, for example, read books and documents. Actually, I very much enjoy this stage because I still think that it will all turn out exactly as I imagined, and I always imagine something really wonderful. This groundwork gives rise to ideas, which would not otherwise have occurred to me. These ideas can be about individual chapters, characters or narrative form, or about quite specific uses of technique. These kinds of ideas can certainly be induced by working. The original idea, though, is only inspired by living one's life with a particular type of commitment. After this comes the stage when everything you do, read, hear, see and think is about the subject you are working on. It develops a kind of radioactive force which 'energizes' everything around it, even things which seeem completely neutral.

Joachim Walther: *No doubt you've come across the kind of mystification that sees the writer as the mouthpiece of some nebulous spirit. The author's voice is not his own but the spirit speaking through him, whispering to him....*

We really have rid ourselves of this mystical illusion. I don't think any of us would believe we were a mouthpiece for 'something or other'. It's quite dramatic in itself to have the sense of being in the grip of something ... Ingeborg Bachmann called this being caught in the strong current of the present. You are clinging to something which won't let you go. It is a thing you personally have to do but at the same time you hope it is of general interest. You are always conscious, though, of the fact that it is you who are writing what you yourself see, hear or feel, that it is you yourself, and not a spirit with this or that thought or opinion.

Joachim Walther: *Is this mystification nurtured perhaps by the fact that one is sometimes baffled by one's own writing? It may contain things one thinks one has never consciously thought deeply about....*

Certainly. That is one of the fundamental experiences in the creative process. But there is nothing mystical about it, it is something which occurs in my brain without my knowledge. Various nerve endings probably start transmitting messages to each other. When you are dreaming you realize that all the levels of your conscious and unconscious are being stirred. That is what I mean by restlessness. This then begins to effervesce and tingle. It's like a great charge which, if you're lucky, will yield some pleasant results in the end. Actually, I increasingly feel that writing is not about creating something original but exposing something whose structure already exists, proceeding, not with hammer and chisel in hand, but very cautiously so as not to cause damage. Mysticism has lingered so long because the material creative processes going on in the brain are very difficult to examine.

Joachim Walther: *It is possible to draw an analogy between the writer's way of working and the scientist's, except that writers do not either prove or disprove their hypothesis in the last sentence of the book. The action does not build up to a grand finale. How does the author manage to hold the reader's attention to the end?*

From the beginning, I know what the fate of the 'hero' will be, and I don't try to conceal this from the reader either. This is not what really interests me. What does interest me is how the character gets there. Whilst I'm working I never think about how I am going to handle the ending. The basic facts are already fixed. What is interesting is how I'll work them out, how I'll tackle them, what relationship I'll build up with my characters, what I'll do with them and what they will do with me. I feel myself developing as they develop. What is important is whether or not I manage to free myself from them: if I don't, then the operation has failed, I have not been able to express everything I wanted to. The factual elements of the plot are of only minor importance. I know them and they don't excite me. Even as a child I was bored by Karl May and read Lessing's plays instead: Why did Emilia's father kill her?*

Joachim Walther: *Even if the factual elements of the plot are fixed, isn't it still possible that the addition of the internal relationships creates a second plot, as you are forced to go back through the various layers of motivation?*

That could happen, if you had a completely free hand in the treatment of your characters. But if you have developed characters by deliberately binding yourself to quite specific authentic events, then it can't. An important problem for me in my writing at the moment is how to combine the authentic aspects of a character which are firmly fixed, with the freedom I

*The reference is to Lessing's play, *Emilia Galotti* – Tr.

am allowed by the fact that I am writing about him or her, by the fact, in other words, that I demarcate the boundaries within which modification can occur. I think this approach is productive and realistic. It is always a question of reappraising the past. When one uses processes whose outcome is known, excitement is aroused not by what happens but by how it happens and why characters act as they do. Hitherto there has been no reason for me to think that I have been driven by the factual details of the plot or that my intention has been altered. (Or perhaps it has? Does somebody's death count as a 'factual detail of the plot'?) Naturally, when you are writing you feel (and it is nice to feel this) that it is growing almost spontaneously. Maybe it has to be like that. But I never forget that it is me it is growing inside, or that I am the one sitting at the typewriter, making it work. I don't fall into a kind of trance. Nor do I lose my self-control, or control over my main characters.

Joachim Walther: *There is one writer whom I suspect you must particularly like – I'm thinking of Büchner, and his novella* Lenz.

Yes, absolutely! That was my first great formative experience in German literature. For me, German prose begins with Büchner's *Lenz*. It is my absolute ideal of prose writing. It was a long time before anyone matched that achievement.

I think it is essential that the writer of modern prose must still be seen and heard through all the fiction and the illusion – which literature cannot and will not give up. That is not an easy demand to satisfy. It is probably easier to construct a story. Perhaps, I don't know, I can only really speak for myself. I remember how it used to be. The plot would be argued over for hours on end. No! she can't marry him. He must start work first, then get to know her, then he must go to the Party secretary who tells him that he is right, he should go back to her, and so on . . . . But that has nothing to do with art. We all realise that now. Writers must stand up and be counted, not hide from the reader behind their fictions; the reader should see the author too.

Joachim Walther: *By switching the focus to inner experiences, aren't you in danger of losing a lot of potential appeal? Aren't you really putting off those readers who want a good story?*

Yes. Those readers are, I believe, increasingly turning to film and television. I have nothing against that, I don't feel superior in any way. But that doesn't change the fact that real prose is something quite different. It should do what it alone can do. This need not necessarily be 'switching the emphasis to inner processes' .... Why do authors exist at all, if they vanish, if they dissolve into what at bottom is a highly abstract and mechanistic fiction that claims to reflect reality? I mean there never has been an author truly able to 'reflect' reality, has there? Reflection is a physical and mechanical process. In this sense there can be no reflection in art, it's more a matter of transforming, appropriating reality. Heiner Müller's comment in one of his plays, that for human beings it is the indecipherable which is lethal, clarified a lot for me. I agree with him. What has not been named and described cannot be present in our social consciousness. And that is what prose should be doing: deciphering the indecipherable, taking what people have not yet seen or experienced, or not yet thought through, and showing it, giving it a name, thinking it through and enabling people to make it their own (that would really make literature a 'force of production'!).

Joachim Walther: *Isn't one of the hallmarks of good literature the fact that it can be appreciated on several levels? That those who are looking for a good read find it, but that those who are seeking the motivations and the reflections behind the action will find something too?*

I don't want to argue that this is not useful to us as an ideal. But there could come a time when a large number of readers won't necessarily demand a strong plot, but something else perhaps. I don't disagree with your remark that a book ought to have different levels to it, but I do think that this is rarely the case in practice, at least in current literature and current literary appreciation. I couldn't sit down and say to myself: right, you must handle this material in such a way that you are able to reach both those who are looking for a good story and those who expect intellectual finesse!

Contemporary conditions do not endow great heroes and great, simple events with popular appeal as easily as did certain archaic mythical paradigms, or situations of great turbulence and severe external conflict, such as war, fascism or class struggle. In such times there was a polarisation of attitudes and action: their importance was unambiguous, indeed it was a matter of life and death. Today, by contrast, decisions and conflicts tend to take place on the plane of social morality, though they are rooted in concrete social movements. A person who is dying inwardly is not generally a spectacular thing. It is not something we can 'see'. Sometimes there are junctures when it can be made visible, but it is really an insidious inner process which is difficult to describe through epiphenomenal developments of plot. Interpolating your own reflections when you are dealing with this kind of material is not therefore mere capriciousness on the part of the author.

Joachim Walther: *Cannot a high degree of reflection in fact yield something quite simple? There is a kind of simplicity which gives rise to something complex, though it goes about it in a very simple way.*

I won't deny this is possible. At the moment, though, I don't think one could reflect on our society and our time from a naive level of consciousness, as one of Grimmelhausen's characters might have done .... Brecht was able to reduce bourgeois society to formulaic statements, even when it had reached a very advanced stage. It may be that as society matures and authors reach a higher vantage point, another opportunity will arise to produce allegories of our times, to write things simply again, to reduce 'it' – everything that now seems to be complicated and confused, and as a result can also appear complicated in literature – to a formula. I'm certainly not in favour of deliberately complicating literature.

My hope is that if I write down as precisely and clearly as possible those thoughts and ideas that spring from the material (after thoroughly reviewing them not only for their personal but also for their social meaningfulness), then there will be a good number of readers willing, and undoubtedly able, to appreciate the process which has led me to use a specific technique and form in my writing. This trust has been vindicated. The complexity of narrative form, however, remains a problem. Some things cannot be expressed simply.

Joachim Walther: *What gives you unpleasant moments when you are writing and what gives you pleasure?*

The basic pleasure I get from writing, which guarantees that I will never give it up, is probably the realisation that it allows me to create the living-space best suited to my needs. Alright, self-fulfilment sounds a bit of a cliché, but don't writers, and all other artists, have the advantage over other people (nowadays, even over most scientists) that their work is personally specific to them and cannot be done by anyone else? I also derive enormous joy from diagnosing social processes from their symptoms. This is basically what motivates me, and hopefully it won't change. Then of course, when I'm actually working on particular things, there are many individual moments of great pleasure.

I've just got over an extremely unenjoyable period, a creative block. Sometimes you can write for weeks, but feel you are treading water. I know then that there must be a block somewhere inside me, though it is one I can't identify at the time. I am somehow resisting getting to the bottom of what the subject matter is driving towards. Obviously, when you write, you are afraid of what will emerge. Nobody voluntarily releases their anxiety. But you must do so as you explore the limits of your subject matter. You must overcome your fear and this is basically only possible through writing. These are the times when I have intensely unpleasurable feelings and of course suffer a great deal of self-doubt. You are dealing with things that you really ought to know, but want neither to know nor admit. You listen to what others are saying, perhaps even to the majority opinion, instead of trusting your own eyes. We are laying bare even deeper levels of our consciousness, and pushing back the frontiers of what we know about ourselves – what society knows about itself, but also, what I know about myself. That is very demanding, but liberating at the same time.

Joachim Walther: *Aren't you running the risk of making yourself ill? By demanding too much of yourself, constantly wanting more than you have achieved, constantly wanting to think what has previously not been thought, you can overtax your own capacity. If you rein in your capacities 'sensibly', there is a greater probability of creating something rounded, your health is spared and any debilitating sense of dissatisfaction is avoided. Is this a question of temperament, or would you see it differently?*

It comes down to your own working experience, how well you know yourself. I mean, you can also work even if you are ill – in order to cure yourself. Writing can be a kind of therapy. I'm not advocating an esoteric or neurotic literature, but we ought not to be frightened of portraying neuroses. I don't think that writing about pathogenic subject-matter is destructive; in fact, it has a healing effect, though obviously only if it is done with the necessary caution, not with brute force.

Joachim Walther: *What is your attitude towards public recognition?*

Public recognition has at least two sides to it. There is one side which no normal person is averse to. With writers, however, the question immediately arises as to whether the recognition results from an appreciation of what they intended or from a misunderstanding – whether the recognition granted them is not actually a misrecognition. Moreover, even if you were not publicly recognised, you could still do nothing other than what you were capable of and felt bound to do. Even if you incur constant displeasure, you cannot suddenly become a different person with different interests or a different style. It's simply not possible.

Constant official publicity, however, is often confused with real social recognition. It is precisely in periods when you are not constantly hearing your own name that you can live very intensely and get to know your own society from a side which perhaps at other times was inaccessible to you. If you become dependent on your name being on everyone's lips, then you are lost. That kind of dependency can be the ruin of you. Wanting to have influence, but not being able to, is extremely hard. It is an experience, though, which arises from living in society and which, if developed correctly, can help you understand the basic principles of your own society and what lies behind them. It is an experience that, had you floated through life on the wings of success, you would never have had. You do not write to become successful. Literature today still contains achievements which remain unrecognized. That is what makes literary figures seem so suspect to those who are successful in other fields. The opposite may also be true: these days, you can see the way writers' self-confidence has sunk very low as the logic of success has been instilled into them, the way the lack of immediate success makes them extremely nervous, the way they develop inferiority complexes and fear that if they are not famous, they will cease to exist. Without these superficial markers of success, literature might have a slower, quieter, and yet more profound influence.

Joachim Walther: *But that requires a considerable amount of self-confidence, if not indeed a belief that one has a personal mission....*

No! Not at all. I cannot imagine that writers today could come to see themselves as having some kind of mission. All that is required is a healthy attitude to oneself, which members of our generation (and here I am no exception) rarely have, and a reasonable opinion of one's own worth. You certainly don't have to think you're one of the greats. Of course this can be a real worry. Writers who are not great cannot rely on their as yet unpublished work retaining its importance in the coming years. That's the crux of the matter. That's why the nervousness and the desire to rush into print set in and being nervous does not improve the quality of one's writing.

Joachim Walther: *Is the root of the trouble perhaps that you always see yourself in relation to other authors and are always looking up towards those who seem in a higher position?*

Exactly, like a system of communicating tubes in a laboratory. It happens completely spontaneously. But I think that it is quite natural, as long as you always judge your temporary rises and falls on the ladder of success calmly and clearly – not with false modesty, but obviously not with hubris either. For a few years now it has been very clear that we have a stable stock of writers who have been constantly improving.

Joachim Walther: *What would you say were the goals of literature under socialism? Are they new ones, or are those which have existed for centuries still valid, provided the concrete form they take is adapted to the current historical situation?*

I don't think that the goals of literature change every five years. With time, writers probably become more keenly attuned to what their own aims are. It may be that society gives writers goals they cannot attain, because they are inappropriate ones for literature; or, on the contrary, society may encourage them to tackle the problems they themselves feel to be their personal concern.

I would like to see literature analysing the conditions in which human beings can realize their own potential as moral beings. This was Bobrowski's theme: how must the world be constituted for a moral being? I don't consider this to be merely one among several tasks for socialist authors; it is their contribution to creating the basic conditions necessary to ensure that the human race neither blows itself up nor otherwise destroys itself. Writers ought, then, to analyse these conditions, regardless of any immediate problems they encounter in the process, and introduce the characters they have discovered or created to such conditions and experiment with them. What writers observe or discover from this must be expressed and written without any inhibition or fear that it could harm their own society. They must start out with the conviction that everything which is said truthfully is useful to society, since it is society itself which has set this goal, and that if they go wrong others are there to correct them. Socialist society and socialist literature share a common goal: the self-realization of the members of society. In seeking to achieve that goal, socialist literature can, temporarily, take on a moralistic, or even didactic, character. But we should aim for lightness and poise in the treatment of our material and in our technique. We should, at all events, avoid being boring.

Joachim Walther: *How fixed are your views? Can we still take you at your word today on things you wrote about years ago?*

Views last only as long as the circumstances they spring from. You may always be taken at your word, though: that is an occupational hazard. Some of my earlier texts I would now write differently, because new experiences have led me to form a different opinion on the subject concerned. This is not so much the case with my literary work, which must always be dependent on the author's own development, but more with my articles and reviews, which were based on a particular attitude towards literature which was widespread at the time – an uncreative, purely ideological approach to literary criticism. These are essays which I would obviously not like to see republished, but I cannot, and would not want to, disown them. They are part of my development. What is crucial is that what you said at the time was sincerely meant, that your mistakes were honest ones (not that this absolves you of them) rather than products of opportunism, which is all-corrupting.

Joachim Walther: *What are the concerns at the heart of your work?*

I am interested in the path of development that mankind has embarked on today in order to ensure its own survival and, if possible, more than mere survival, in the tensions which arise between social groups and the individual in this process, and in how these can ultimately be employed to produce humanity rather than destruction.

Joachim Walther: *And you think that this depends essentially on morality?*

No, morality does not exist as an autonomous institution. It depends rather on whether people create the conditions that enable them to discover themselves, whether they can find an interest in themselves – interest in the sense of active interest in their own lives, freed of course of all mystification – that will cause them to regard themselves as sufficiently important, exciting and valuable that they will do everything possible to save themselves. In my opinion this hasn't yet been resolved. Literature provides one opportunity for keeping people's interest in themselves alive, or rekindling it. At this point, the question which arises for the prose writer is, interest in what? In what subject? And probably for some time to come I will see this as the key problem facing our generation, and one that is obviously close to my own heart. I am concerned with what this generation has tried to do, what it has succeeded in, but also what it has failed in and what successes have been denied it. I am concerned with what we owe this generation, but also what it owes others, and, of course, what it yearns for, and what it is capable of, both for good and evil. Then, very importantly, I am interested in how it perceives itself, which would prove whether or not its most conscious and important representatives have succeeded in reaching maturity, or whether it has remained at a certain stage of immaturity, and is seeking to excuse itself. I mean, what kind of shape its conscience is in. This demands strenuous questioning and self-questioning. I don't think that my generation is more important than those that come either before or after it. I merely think that no-one older or younger could say what has been important for our generation. And, naturally, one also hopes that the experience of one's own generation is of interest to others.

Joachim Walther: *I'd like to ask you one or two questions about style. If I am correct, you are using fewer and fewer adjectives. Adjectives tend to narrow down an idea, making it more vivid and immediate. Strangely enough, the near-total absence of adjectives from your work has not diminished its graphic qualities. How does this come about? Are you replacing external description with some kind of inner exactitude which serves to give a vividness to externals?*

I have not consciously been using fewer adjectives, but, now you mention it, you are probably right. This could well be because I have moved away from description understood as a simple describing of objects, and from milieu as merely incidental background to action or conversation. I am trying to make the setting, everything which belongs to the characters in a spatial sense, a part of them. I don't mean just seeing it through their eyes but letting it in some way take an active part, so that it is not just there as background or supplementary detail, as stage scenery or decoration. This may have made me use adjectives more carefully, as one also trains oneself to do when one realizes that simply amassing adjectives does not necessarily make one's style more graphic. This is what I have come to learn. A concept which is in itself very general, let's take 'sky' as an example, doesn't necessarily have to be further qualified by an adjective of colour or atmosphere. It is rather that, from the setting or the situation in which the word 'sky' occurs, the context created should assign the word a very specific emotional and atmospheric value, i.e. an aesthetic value, even though one reader may picture this sky as grey and another may imagine it to be blue.

Joachim Walther: *You seem to have begun to use dialogue very sparingly too. Are you deliberately avoiding it?*

Yes, I have concentrated more on indirect speech – though I don't avoid dialogue entirely. The indirect speech and style I use is held together by a specific authorial voice, which I never seek to conceal. The author speaks directly and interacts in every conceivable way with the characters, thus opening up many more possibilities than if I were simply to depend on the 'he said . . .', 'she said . . .' technique. It seems to me that in modern prose, the author is duty bound to allow readers to share in the creation of fiction, rather than simply setting it down in front of them as a second reality outside reality. Incidentally, this is the most difficult thing to express, as it is the thing one is least conscious of. This attitude towards both the subject matter and the reader has a far-reaching influence on one's style.

Joachim Walther: *How important do you consider detail to be? Chekhov demanded that if a pistol was hanging on the wall, then it should go off, and that it should do so during the story. Do you think that every detail must have a direct and identifiable function? Or do you see chance as also being functional in a story?*

As I said earlier, I am very much against structuring what I write too rigidly. To exclude chance altogether runs entirely counter to the spirit of art. Not even a scientist would do that. There is of course a vast amount of detail which could find its way into the story as pure description. Here you must choose; you can't include it all. I see another form of chance at work here, concerning which details you leave out and which you incorporate. Not that I would say that the reason why you think certain things are significant and worth mentioning can simply be put down to chance. It is not that you do it consciously, but neither is it pure chance; it is an unconscious selection. It is fundamentally mistaken to equate literature and nature, to think that you are simply taking a slice of nature and transferring it onto paper. A subjective choice is always involved.

Joachim Walther: *By what criteria do you assess the quality of literature?*

It would be difficult to sum that up in a word. What it boils down to is really whether you get a sense of it speaking to one's time. The feeling that you are holding some kind of radioactive material in your bare hands, or better, with the appropriate instruments. The feeling that a spark has come over, that something has touched that part of me, the reader, which is also radioactive. So it is not a question of style or form, but more the way in which we grasp our world and are then in turn gripped by it. But the book has also, of course, to be well written to produce this feeling.

Joachim Wather: *You have a reputation as a writer for delving where it hurts most, even if it causes you pain yourself.*

If this is right, then it is something that I can't change, that I can't resolve either to do or not to do. It is because my concern is always with what I feel to be a sensitive spot at any particular moment. And others feel this too sometimes – if I'm lucky. This is, of course, where the argument begins as to whether one should just let these old wounds heal over in peace or whether they should, in fact, be re-opened in order to encourage the formation of antibodies within society which will help in the healing process. That is a dilemma which will never be resolved. Which will always flare up again each time someone touches a sensitive spot. I think this is quite normal. But for myself and for my own work, I have resolved the dilemma.

Joachim Walther: *In your volume of essays, you write that the narrative sphere has four dimensions, three being fictional and concerned with the characters one has created and a fourth, which you describe in great depth and with great commitment, which concerns the deep involvement of the author with the material, the virtual identity of author and ego. Could this not be the source of the mystery of the poetical: the fourth dimension being beyond human imagination.*

What I believe is that once writers stop putting everything into what they are writing, holding nothing back, then the poetic probably vanishes. I can't claim, though, that the poetic is born only in this way nor that this is all it consists of. There must be much more to this nebulous concept of the poetical, things which are difficult to define, but quite real. If one were to restrict oneself to the first three planes only – to the fictional characters acting out a fabricated plot – then one would produce something very shallow. Depth, by which I really mean poetic effect, arises from the author adding his or her time and commitment, which gives the work a fourth dimension. Maybe that's not expressed very well, but something indefinable is produced, which one can sense immediately.

Joachim Walther: *Aren't we in fact observing an elementary poetic process when a child gives names to things beyond the limits of its comprehension?*

Absolutely, this is probably where it begins. You can see how children, when they play, try to express themselves by inventing a game which at the time helps them cope with a real-life occurrence. They can work this through in their games and it becomes assimilable as experience. When a child gives something a name, puts familiar words together in a new arrangement, or dreams up something completely new, this must be seen as a poetic process. It is not merely a cognitive process; though poetry is also cognition, but not in rationalistic form.

Joachim Walther: *Certainly that is not all there is to the poetic, but one could perhaps get close to it by analogy. Couldn't one see oneself constantly as a child faced with the as yet unnamed?*

I suppose one could. That's something one ought to consider. What you are saying is precisely what I think too, namely that every poetic utterance is basically a creative process, that there is no inherent reason why we should call a bin a 'bin', why we should take over this convention, this labelling scheme. For a child, a bin can be a tent or indeed anything else. If it sees it as such, it has created something new, something which did not previously exist. At least this is a part of it. It isn't all there is to it, but the starting point perhaps. Yet it is precisely this uninhibited way of looking at things which is difficult for us as adults.

Joachim Walther: *Do you have a vision of what you would like to achieve?*

Yes, I do. Perhaps a very common one .... Basically I would like literature, or what I can express in literature, to drain every ounce of my energy. I would like, in the end, to have been able fully to express my experiences and insights, my own constant development and attempts to define my position in this age, without being left with the usual residue of the unsaid and the unsayable. It is, of course, unattainable.

October 1972

2

SUBJECTIVE AUTHENTICITY

A Conversation with Hans Kaufmann*

Hans Kaufmann: *In the section entitled 'Tabula Rasa' in your essay 'The Reader and the Writer'* (Lesen und Schreiben), *you try to arrive at a clear understanding of the role books, or rather 'prose' – something I'd like to come back to – play, by imagining what your life would have been like if there had been none and you had not even known of the existence of the* Grimms' fairy tales, Gulliver's Travels, Wilhelm Meister *or* Anna Karenina. *'Without books,' you conclude, 'I am not me.' By examining your own experiences, you try to present a kind of empirical argument to counter the fear – which you express in the section of the essay entitled 'Lament' – that as the sciences, communications technology, film, radio and television increasingly enter into our lives, contemporary literature, and especially prose, might lose its purpose. I'd also like to mention the part of the essay you call 'Rough Outline for a Writer', where you discuss the social status of 'literary artisans' in the GDR, compare their situation with that of writers living under capitalism, and at the same time highlight the moral risks run by those who make their living from writing. I believe, by the way, that too little attention is given to this subject in public literary debate.*

Yes, but as you know that is beginning to change, because in recent years authors like Günter de Bruyn, Jurek Becker, Erwin Strittmatter and Anna Seghers, for example, have begun to debate the ethical issues raised by their professional activity.

Hans Kaufmann: *Leaving aside the other, equally significant, points the essay makes about history, literary theory and epistemology, would this be a more or less fair summary of what you say there: in order to firm up the*

*Originally published in *Weimarer Beiträge*, no. 6 (East Berlin 1976).

conviction that writing prose was worthwhile, you had to subject that
conviction to doubt, and in so doing, you were also able to show the sense –
and necessity – of writing a specific kind of literature which you felt at the
time – and which you perhaps still feel – to be relevant?

I can only write about things that disturb me. I wrote 'The Reader and the
Writer' in 1968. I had finished *The Quest for Christa T.* a year before, but
it had not yet been published, though the first critical reactions to it had
given me a good idea of what the tone of public criticism would be. So at
the time I wasn't so bothered about anything as pompous and general as
'the fate of the novel'. The book would run its own course, irrespective of
what I thought about it. Nor did I see any reason to justify myself in any
way. But I did feel a need to re-appraise my experience of writing the
book, and so I set out to articulate my feelings, at the same time asking
myself what was uniquely significant about a book, and which aspects of
it could be used again in future works. To that extent, there is not a fundamental difference between the prose and the essay aspects of my work –
the one follows on from the other, they are intertwined. The root they
share is that of an experience which needs to be assimilated: experience of
'life', by which I mean experience of the tangible reality of a particular
time in a particular society; experience of myself, of writing – which is an
important part of my life, of other literatures and art. Prose and the essay
are two different tools used to tackle different types of material for different, though not opposed or mutually exclusive ends.

In any case, in both genres you start completely from scratch; it isn't
like the hedgehog entering the race with the hare, secure in the knowledge
that his wife will be waiting at the finishing post to squeak 'I'm already
here'. Having defined prose for myself and recognising it as the form most
suitable for me, I was not sure whether I would become more convinced of
the point of writing it when I began to inquire whether it was – or at least
could be – really appropriate for modern times. I must admit, by the way,
that in the long run there was no question of my not carrying on writing,
whatever the result of my inquiry, though I might have started to write
differently. This kind of soul-searching has, in some way, to be ruthless,
even with axioms that you take for granted and hold dear. An example of
one such axiom is that socialist authors do not need to worry about the
state of the novel; that they can quite comfortably leave that to those
writers who are embroiled in the capitalist literary business, who are
forced to grapple with the bourgeois novel in its terminal state.

But why should I be asking these questions? Because as a reader I rarely
come across a novel written here that concerns me? Because I fear that our
prose writing fails to expresss the problems that many people – even entire
social strata – face in their lives? Even though I am increasingly coming

across work that is well-written, polished and has artistic merit. But show me a book that sears into you as life itself does. That you can't find.

Any debate about the life and death of the novel starts and finishes there. If it can no longer excite me, then it deserves to die! Now, the parts of the essay you mentioned deal with the conditions in which prose as a genre can survive, and in doing so, they refer to the domains that prose has 'lost' during its historical development. Yet the history of art is not a history of wars; its gains and losses can't be described in the language of the General Staff; its territory can't be measured in square miles; there are no devices for assessing its effects. Strangely enough, writers of my own and younger generations react to these simple and indisputable facts with uneasy consciences. This comes out – if it isn't already apparent – in the way they seek to defend themselves (a way I am very used to, may I add) by themselves adopting their critics' misguided notions, protesting that they simply want the same as everyone else (which is not true), and ending up merely trying to prove their worth in areas where literature has never lost anything, and hence has nothing to gain either. So, when I wrote the essay, I wanted to express my opinion of what prose can and should do.

Hans Kaufmann: *Can we insert a snippet of biography here? From a letter Louis Fürnberg wrote to you in 1956, a year before he died, I deduce that you had told him of your intention to work as a writer, at the same time expressing your doubts and reservations. Fürnberg encouraged you with great passion. Could you say something about the motives behind your decision to enter the world of literary production?*

I had been 'writing' for ages – mainly diaries in the early days, but also folk-tales, 'short stories', even drafts of 'plays'. Looking back, I was irritated by my German studies, and moved into criticism and theory – I wrote literary criticism. Perhaps I had lost a degree of immediacy in my contact with reality, as well as the carefree spirit that is necessarily part of the decision to throw caution to the winds and add one's own two-penny-worth to the mountain of words already written. Anyway, I was faced with serious obstacles which needed a great deal of shaking before they could be overcome and before the urge to write could be released. Louis Fürnberg was wonderfully good at encouraging people, even when he didn't have much to be encouraged by. I think of him when someone who is just beginning to write gives me a manuscript to read. These days, by the way, young people don't seem to be writing prose . . . .

Hans Kaufmann: *Let's talk about 'prose'. Allow me to indulge in a little crude philology. Citing Thomas Mann, you call the 'prose author' the one who 'murmurs the spell of the imperfect'. Yet that was how Thomas Mann described the* Erzähler *– the story-writer – whom he understood in the more or less 'traditionalist' sense. Is the distinction meaningless in your eyes? If it is, we can drop the subject, but I do suspect that your essay deliberately avoids terms like 'narrative literature' or 'epic', preferring 'the prose genre'. Its generic features, you say, are that it is written by individuals (a fate it shares with the major part of poetry and most drama) and read by individuals (which is indeed especially true of prose literature). Now, in 1961 your 'Moscow Novella' was published, a short work whose very title puts it in a particular category; 'The Divided Heaven' (1963) is called an* Erzählung, *a short story. You didn't assign* The Quest for Crista T. *(1968) to any particular genre. Is it true to say that on the one hand the word 'prose' – as far as critical considerations of a general kind are concerned – refers to more or less any type of narrative literature, but that, on the other – insofar as it suggests an idea of a particular objective – it means a very special type of style which you are loath to connect with any idea of 'story-telling', because – taking* Quest for Christa T. *for instance – it is a combination of biographical and autobiographical details, critical observations and documentation, and is, in essence, built of reflections?*

You're right. When I wrote the essay I noticed that the distinction between 'story-teller' and 'prose writer' was not insignificant. It was not by chance that I took up this idea of a writer who 'murmurs the spell of the imperfect', a formulation I find wonderful; and I had reason to question a remark – made by Anna Seghers – to which I subscribed, and which seemed to be confirmed by my earlier experience of writing: what has become narratable is already mastered. You see, I had learned – and I must say I learned to my surprise, and despite my own considerable unwillingness to accept it – what it really meant to have to tell the story of someting in order to master it. I had found that story-writers – or perhaps I should say prose writers – can be compelled to abandon the strict sequence of first living through something, then digesting and 'mastering' it and, lastly, writing about it. In order to achieve the inner authenticity for which they are striving, they can be forced to express the living and thinking processes they are embroiled in directly in their work process, in an almost unmitigated way (though form always does tone things down, that is one of its functions). They can be forced to drop all artificial categories, empty moulds into which, almost always with the unconscious help of the author, the raw material pours with alarming inevitability.

Am I making myself clear? I would be so delighted if, when I expressed my thoughts on these questions, I were not seen as relapsing into some kind of ecstasy or taking refuge in the inaccessible recesses of the so-called artistic labour-process. Yet this new spontaneity, which I believed had almost been lost forever, had burst to the surface in such a tangible, liberating way that I would have been ill-advised to underestimate its value or to recoil from it in fear. (And this also meant I could very quickly recognise what was worthy of criticism in the product of this labour-process.)

In saying this, I am well aware that 'inner authenticity' is not a literary category that means something to everyone, like 'positive hero', 'conflict', 'the comic' or even 'plot' (by the way, the German word for 'plot', *Fabel*, used to mean a made-up story, as opposed to 'true account'). In this sense, the plot can on occasion be an obstacle to creating precisely that inner authenticity (genuineness, credibility) which you can immediately spot – though you may find it hard to define – in a piece of prose writing. This, however you look at it, is the opposite of the positivist approach that separates author and subject-matter and counterposes the one to the other. In that approach, authors have to proceed as though they were using a kind of lasso, with which they must haul in their poor subject-matter and then interpret it. They can either be on foot or on horseback, clumsy cowboys or expert ones, casual or hard-working. However they go about it, when they show us their catch, they are still the same people as when they started out. And then they make so bold as to hope their readers will have been 'changed' by reading the book!

Recently a friend advised me not to get bogged down in a polemic against 'plot'. That, he said, could become as dogmatic as glorifying it. He's right: this is not the crux of the argument. Let me quote Erasmus here, as a precaution: 'Everything I say is merely conversation. None of it is advice. I would not speak so boldly, were people supposed to act upon what I said.' What I mean is that I am only speaking for myself when I confess that in writing of that kind, I was struck by an element of dishonesty that increasingly worried me: namely, the unfortunate possibility authors have of sheltering behind their 'material', 'subject', 'work' or whatever; of turning that work into something they can play around with at will (and of thus treating readers as objects too); of ending up with a piece of work which took x number of hours to write, which can be reproduced by technical means, and then sold as a commodity. (A developed socialist society will have to question the commodity character of intellectual work.)

To my mind, it is much more useful to look at writing, not as an end product, but as a process which continuously runs alongside life, helping to shape and interpret it: writing can be seen as a way of being more intensely involved in the world, as the concentration and focusing of thought, word and deed. It is also a process that gives rise to certain printable by-products (from which, last but not least, the writer can earn a living). These represent the material evidence of a productivity that is mainly oriented towards the creation of new structures of human relations in the present, in other words towards something that is not material, and yet intensely real and meaningful.

This mode of writing is not 'subjectivist', but 'interventionist'. It does require subjectivity, and a subject who is prepared to undergo unrelenting exposure – that is easy to say, of course, but I really do mean as unrelenting as possible – to the material at hand, to accept the burden of the tensions that inexorably arise, and to be curious about the changes that both the material and the author undergo. The new reality you see is different from the one you saw before. Suddenly, everything is interconnected and fluid. Things formerly taken as 'given' start to dissolve, revealing the reified social relations they contain and no longer that hierarchically arranged social cosmos in which the human particle travels along the paths pre-ordained by sociology or ideology, or deviates from them. It becomes more and more difficult to say 'I', and yet at the same time often imperative to do so. I would like to give the provisional name 'subjective authenticity' to the search for a new method of writing which does justice to this reality. I can only hope I have made it clear that this method not only does not dispute the existence of objective reality, but is precisely an attempt to engage with 'objective reality' in a productive manner.

One more thing. When I say 'authenticity', I don't mean 'truthfulness'; I'm not moralising. Truthfulness must be taken for granted; it is absolutely undeniable that literature cannot exist without it. This is also true in a wider sense, because the unfortunate outcome of remaining in artistic blindness and ignorance and attempting to be 'truthful' from only a restricted point of view, is provincialism. Similarly, that form of retreat which seeks to keep one's own inner passions apart from the burning issues of the day causes your creativity to wane and you're left with the kind of artistic activity about which nothing bad can be said apart from the fact that nobody – particularly its producer – feels it to be necessary.

Hans Kaufmann: *I would like to return to the idea of experience. I realise, of course, that the artist cannot give shape to any object or process that takes his fancy, which has no bearing on him. His work expresses the personal relationship he, as an individual human being, has with the world; he cannot present a world devoid of subjects. You're aiming at something similar by insisting adamantly on experience. On the other hand, the idea is undeniably elastic and amorphous, and hence has little philosophical value. There is always the great danger that 'experience' is, rightly or wrongly, understood in the empiricist sense that an individual can only relate to what he or she receives from the sensible environment. For this reason, I would like us to remember that around the turn of the century, literature began to discover that (empirical) experience was not, or was no longer, adequate for portraying the determining factors in individuals' lives, and that these were to be found 'in the invisible', as a despairing Rilke put it. Later on, Brecht put the debate on a decisively more realist course by rejecting the notion of 'milieu' and arguing that it should be replaced by that of the 'causal social nexus'. In order to make conscious the dialectic between determination and individual freedom of action, factors relating to society in its entirety have to be considered, which, while they are beyond sensory experience, are very real. (It is precisely for this reason that the break with nineteenth-century realism is both justified and necessary.) It is still true today, is it not, that the only way of comprehending the reality and scope of individuality is through the causal nexus, which, though it has in some respects undergone change, is far from inoperative?*

You're touching on such a fundamental point that we must get to the bottom of it, even if we have in the end to agree to differ. You are clearly afraid that my 'adamant insistence on experience' might let idealism slip in through the back door – 'Here I am, I can't do anything about it, God help me, Amen'. So for the sake of clarity, I'd like to repeat something I've often said before (including in 'The Reader and the Writer'). Marxist philosophy is one of my fundamental experiences, and plays a decisive role in the selection and evaluation of new experiences; writers living in an age when they can choose the way they wish to write, are responsible for the content of their experience; finally, writing from experience is not the same as always describing oneself (though self-depiction often does and will come into it). In other words, none of this has anything to do with what might be called 'unfettered subjectivism', which may obscure rather than illuminate reality (of which the writer is part).

Yet have you ever realised how steeped in unfettered subjectivism are those who urge authors to write in accordance with idealised images and theoretical constructs rather than from experience? No, it is still, and always will be, a question of realism and the fight for it. And this fight, which led Brecht (for a time) to place emphasis – and it is an emphasis I cannot quibble with – on the social ties in which individuals are embedded, and the interplay between social and individual factors, part of this fight is that today we – for I am not the only one – take a certain pleasure in insisting on a category, 'experience', that has so long been ignored, underestimated and regarded as suspect, and which appears to give you some cause for alarm. We cannot deny the plain fact that the writer of 'good' literature cannot depict 'the world', or 'reality' or anything so intangible. Writers are not natural scientists, and literature is not a branch of philosophy. As Anna Seghers said, 'The writer is the curious crossing point where object becomes subject and turns back into object.' The reservoir writers draw on in their writing is experience, which mediates between objective reality and the authorial subject. And it is highly desirable that this should be socially meaningful experience, the determinants of which do not reside in 'the invisible'.

Even if 'experience' really were so suspect a philosophical term as you assume, I wouldn't put it any differently, for there still wouldn't be a good case against using the term in a sphere that is distinguished from science and philosophy *precisely* by the importance of the subjective dimension. (This is one of the crucial issues in the argument between Marxist authors and their Marxist critics that has been going on for more than forty years now.) In any case, natural scientists and Marxist philosophers who are concerned with science are now taking the category of 'experience' seriously again. In molecular biology, for example, debate is focusing on whether a molecular system can acquire 'experience', in other words whether it can learn.

Don't worry, I'm not going to overdo the comparison between the regulatory mechanisms of an insensate cell bound by the constraints of biology and an individual consciously living in a set of historical and social relations. But the very fact of historical determination, with which present-day writers should be familiar, ought to prompt them to ask how much scope individuals have for freely-determined action – how far, for example, they are responsible and culpable for inaction in an age of extreme terror. Brecht himself spoke of the 'testing ground of social causality', an arena where various forces are at work. One of these forces is the individual whom we must not paralyse by presenting his or her fate as being exclusively determined by objective, economic factors. If, for a time, Brecht tended to lay emphasis on the social determinants, while the current trend among Marxist writers is to examine the role of the individual in this 'causal nexus', isn't this something we can also explain with the aid of a historical materialist approach?

Hans Kaufmann: *For obvious reasons, the whole of GDR literature has paid a great deal of attention to the analysis of fascism. It isn't only writers of the older and middle generations who write about it; those who were no more than children when liberation came do so too. What might be the reasons for this, and what significance does it have for today's reader? Which major new elements of this subject still have potential for literature?*

The question is closely tied in with what I said before, because I do tackle, well, how can I put it, 'the subject of fascism'. We only have to look at ourselves. A past like fascism envelops us like a wave, unless we put up an internal barrier against it (which is a defence mechanism that is commonly employed). But nobody can evade the effects, or seal themselves off from influences that penetrate from childhood and youth into later life, even when – indeed, especially when – they would prefer to forget and deny (first and foremost deny to themselves) the influences to which they were exposed as children, and the behaviour they acquired. Tracing the maturation process my generation went through, seeing where that process came to a halt, is an enormous subject. Those who grew up under fascism cannot say they had 'got over' it by such and such a date. It is a matter of working through this monstrous – in the true sense of the word – occurrence at ever deeper, and hence ever more personal levels; a process that literature has to pursue, which can also mean 'get at the causes of', perhaps even 'help to resolve'.

It is, moreover, a very difficult thing to do, and the resistance one encounters indicates how radioactive the material still is, even today (another sign is that certain themes related to our childhood never come up in conversation). Perhaps that is why we have become accustomed to describing fascism as a 'phenomenon' which existed outside us and which ceased to be as soon as its centres of power and organizational forms had been destroyed. Have we not for some time now ascribed it to the past of 'the other Germany', so that we can simply regard anti-fascism and resistance as our own traditions? (This, I believe, has also clearly been present throughout the various stages of literary treatment of fascism, particularly if film and television drama are included.) And yet young people are constantly asking why, 'in spite of everything', people like us, their parents, could live through those days without being oppressed by a constant sense of calamity. More importantly, how we were able to carry on living afterwards. In this 'in spite of everything' they are referring to all the films they've seen, all the history they were taught at school about the circumstances surrounding Hitler's take-over. But they have a right to understand it, and we have a duty to answer their questions as best we can.

Apart from the more psychological difficulties involved, which seem to have remained insurmountable for so many years, I would also like just to mention that problems of method also arise. Again, it's a question of finding a style of writing that allows this undertaking a great degree of realism – or even better, imposes that realism upon it – so that past and present can be seen not only to 'meet' on the paper, but, as they constantly do in every one of us, to interact and be endlessly rubbing up against each other. In other words, you have to find writing techniques (and make it known that you are looking for such techniques, and why) that manage to free up those almost indissoluble bonds and constrictions that hold us in their grip, to unravel that vast range of elements that have become entwined during our development, so that patterns of behaviour in which we thought we were firmly entrenched can be explained, and, where possible (and where necessary), still be changed. It's a rather demanding task.

Hans Kaufmann: *I've been struck recently by the way a number of books dealing with the past – the years before or around 1945 for instance – are written with great talent, but the same authors clearly find it hard to portray the dialectical relation in our present day between the opportunities real people have for action and the conditions in which that action takes place. While theory has noisily proclaimed the greater significance of the individual, in practice we are left with really insipid, shallow figures. Alongside this, I have noticed elements of idealist philosophising appearing when writers attempt, in literary theory, aphorisms and other forms of writing, to conceptualise their own present situation and work – and this is true of writers whose socialist convictions cannot be doubted. I even think there is something of this in your writings. I wonder whether these two features – involving, as they often do, conflicts, disappointments and crises – are not connected with the difficulties one has in putting one's own experiences in the context of the overall state of things, of the way things are developing generally. Of course, this is not only an individual concern; it also has to do with the image our society as a whole has of itself – and I shall come back to that in a moment. But how and to what extent the individual becomes aware of this; whether he sets out to recognise the concrete historical, true nature of these moments of crisis; whether he is incapable of or even uninterested in doing so: none of this is inconsequential. Where he fails – for whatever reason – the result is partly that curious emptiness we have seen over the last few years, partly the kind of self-interpretation tinged with idealism that I have just mentioned. (I am talking, by the way, about a few exceptional publications, not about anything like a general trend in modern GDR literature.)*

I'm very glad to hear you speak of 'experience' and the significance of individual assimilation of experience .... I also agree with what you have just said – avoiding contradiction inevitably creates emptiness in literature, because real, concrete movement drops out of the picture and only apparent motion is left.

Hans Kaufmann: *What I'm getting at is that experience has to be supplemented before it can be assimilated. Following Marx and Lenin's indications on the phases of communism, an important contribution was made at the 8th Party Congress* and in the subsequent period, to the definition of developed socialist society and its historical status. It seems to me that we have not given enough thought to what realism in literature can gain from this 'realism' in scientific self-understanding and political praxis, which Erich Honecker spoke of there. For example, the developmental stage we*

---

*This was the Congress of 1971, the year in which Honecker took over – Tr.

consider ourselves to be living in is important – indeed it is crucial – for the form the relationship between the ideal and the real takes in a work of art. If our conceptions and our practice treated socialism as a complete and isolated social formation, things that appear to need criticising – and such things inevitably come to the surface as writers and others observe and get to grips with the lives we lead – would have no historical status; such things would be regarded as merely chance phenomena, abnormal and untypical. Or, alternatively, one would spontaneously be tempted to regard every source of discord as 'evidence' refuting the definition society had given of itself. Either way, we would be lacking a dialectic of contemporary development, and the ideal and reality would be rigidly cast in an irresolvable antinomy, with an emotional, moral and aesthetic overlay.

If, however, bearing in mind the developmental level of the forces and relations of production, we perceive society in terms of the features that cast the last shadows of class antagonism, which still exist even though that antagonism has largely been eradicted, and, more importantly, in terms of its readiness for communism, then we arrive at a quite different way of viewing and evaluating the general significance of individual phenomena. This does not of course mean that the tensions between the ideal and reality dissolve into a harmonious relation; yet they do help us to understand the historical dynamic and thereby to become a subjective force and hence an element in that dynamic itself. Furthermore, any phenomenon that appears undesirable from the point of view of socialist goals does not simply fall out of the 'system'; it loses its abnormal, monstrous and ultimately inexplicable character and is put into historical perspective, which in turns reveals how it might be successfully tackled. The relative and general significance of any source of discontent can then be understood without its acquiring the character of abstract generality, or of a 'bad reality' standing over against a subjective 'good will'. Would this not also do away with the need – which can be problematic – to attribute general validity to one's own, sometimes complex, experiences in intimations, antitheses, allusions and similes? Perhaps we could quote Heinrich Heine here, who said:

> Don't bother with your holy parables,
> Nor with your pious theories,
> Try and answer our damned questions,
> Without beating about the bush.

(Laß die heil'gen Parabolen,
Laß die frommen Hypothesen
Suche die verdammeten Fragen
Ohne Umschweif uns zu lösen.)

That was a long digression on my part, there won't be any more.

Let me express my respect for Heine. Though I must say I'd like to see the look on his face if I showed him some of our 'damned questions' .... But that's by the by. I don't deny the problem you have been broaching exists; indeed I have been aware of it for a long time, occasionally to the point of despair. Anna Seghers was right when she wrote to Georg Luckács thirty-five years ago, in the course of their still very relevant correspondence, that 'fear of deviation has the effect of rendering unreal'. It is indeed the case that if, over a long period of time, you are prevented from doing things openly, you can even forget how to avoid beating about the bush when you ask important – though not always answerable – questions (damned or otherwise), even if you only ask them of yourself. This is true in many fields, but it lies at the very heart of literature. Mechanisms of self-censor-ship are even more dangerous than the censorship from which they develop, for they internalize the kinds of demands that can prevent liter-ature from being created, and bog writers down in a sterile and hopeless web of incompatible codes ordaining, for example, that they should write realistically and yet disregard conflict, that they should faithfully depict the truth and yet disbelieve what they see because what they see is 'un-typical'. A writer who is not acutely aware of this process, who fails to monitor his or her own work implacably, will start to give in, make excuses and produce 'pulp'. And you will do so whether you are writing a period novel, a parable or a utopian work – the genre is immaterial.

There is still some point in talking about this today. Ingrained mechan-isms go on producing effects. It wasn't for nothing that Volker Braun recently asked where our 'reserves of realism' were .... What is it you had in mind when you mentioned elements of idealist philosophising in my work?

Hans Kaufmann: *Is it not possible – and I beg you to treat what I say as a question rather than an assertion – that the unresolved problems of the last few years, which I hinted at, are at the roots of these flashbacks to fascism and to its effects upon our generation? I also suspect that an element of 'intellectual history' is creeping in. But perhaps we should pass over this question, because it really concerns a book that's still being written, and with which I am therefore not fully acquainted.*

Why pass it over? Let's try and get to the bottom of your worries and reservations. Perhaps by formulating my thoughts in a more exact way, I can put your mind at rest a little without having to say too much about my current project. The questions have been put in a sufficiently general manner.

You suspect that my treatment of the fascism theme could involve 'intellectual history', in other words reference merely to the psychological and moral processes in the development of consciousness, and you wish to warn me that the actual reality that lies behind these processes may be left out of account. I agree with you that this shouldn't be allowed to happen. But contemporary authors writing about fascism find themselves in a different environment from anti-fascist writers in exile or just after the war. As time passes, and in this case as our lifetime passes, each period of history is constantly acquiring a new dimension, and this is particularly true of the age of fascism. As a result, the reality that provides me with my material is no longer fascism – its socio-economic roots, the property relations from which it evolved, and so on – but the structure of the relations my generation has with the past; in other words, the way people in the present come to terms with the past. This is something quite different from a procedure of working by analogy; that really would be quite inadmissible. I have no intention of finding an ersatz 'solution' to the difficulties facing literature when it tries to come to terms with the present by turning real contradictions that issue from a concrete social situation into general psychological categories, and thereby concealing them.

In fact, I set out to do just the opposite. I hope to gain access to the present by treating the past in a concrete, historical fashion. As Brecht wrote in 1953: 'We have been all too keen to turn our backs on the immediate past and, hungry with curiosity, to look to the future. But the future will depend on whether we can come to terms with the past.' Perhaps you will agree that Brecht's point about the dialectical relationship between the past and the future is equally valid today.

Hans Kaufmann: *In terms of attitudes to German fascism, things are not exactly as they were in 1953. But the last sentence is undoubtedly still significant.*

Well, quite independently of what Brecht said of course, the deficiencies in this 'coming to terms with the past' became very apparent to me each day as I dealt with, and reflected upon, the problems and, in particular, as I dealt with and thought about the people who created them – and I include myself here. No other generation will ever go through what we did: growing up in and being educated and shaped by one society and then having the opportunity, in the GDR, to express a form of criticism and self-criticism that went right to the very roots of society; being given the chance to think, understand and act, and, as a result, coming up against new, far from simple conflicts and contradictions; and, what is even more important, being involved in creating and resolving those contradictions, while at the same time being unable to disown the model of behaviour that had shaped our childhood and youth. Now try telling me that isn't a contradictory continuum! And of course it is a continuum, because the person who experiences all that is one and the same – or are they the same at the end of it all? Whatever the case, there was no 'zero hour' when they were changed from one person into another . . . .

This is probably what we mean by 'the subject of fascism'. Shouldn't we be permitted, indeed required to get to grips with it? And shouldn't we also be able to take for granted what has been written about it in other types of literature, which, though they adopted a different approach, are still important and valid? What I am asking is, can't we start out from the achievements of earlier generations, the best of which we can call classics, without having to repeat what they did? And start out from the economic and historical analyses our children are taught at school, which were like revelations to us when we first heard them?

I do not believe my attitude to this issue simply reflects my own private feelings, or even my resentment. It seems to me, rather, that it is in society's fundmental interest to see re-established the connection between this part of our lives and the present, which seemed almost to have been lost forever. We will have to talk about property relations; but we should not be wary of enquiring into psychological mechanisms as well. We will have to go through the history that we seem to 'know so well' again and again, without ceasing to be astonished and, I can assure you, horrified at what we find. We will have to resurrect what appeared to be dead and open up that which has become ossified and intractable to abstract analysis. Surprisingly enough, in this case 'to historicise' will not mean 'to alienate', but to draw closer to us a historical period that we had distanced from ourselves and turned into a battlefield of impersonal social forces; it will mean making individuals – in their actions or inaction – visible once again, to inquire into their – our – motives and responsibilities . . . .

Can you call all this intellectual history? Not at all. Rather, it is a self-assured affirmation of the kind of 'interventionist thinking' that Brecht called for as early as 1933. 'The need to criticise fascism as a complex body of modes of behaviour by means of interventionist thinking. To criticise also ideas when they represent interventionist behaviour.' Moreover, it means to attempt to answer new types of questions posed by an audience living in a new and different concrete historical environment.

Hans Kaufmann: *Together with Gerhard Wolf, you wrote the script for a film about Till Eulenspiegel. You set his story among the various struggles that preceded the German Peasant Wars. In the traditional version of the Till Eulenspiegel story, things are, of course, quite different: feudal society is stable, and the hero appears as a bourgeois individual ahead of his time, because he is set off against the rest of society as the only radical in both practical and intellectual terms – for Eulenspiegel, God, the idea of a 'beyond' and redemption, are meaningless. It would also have been possible to cast a contemporary eye on the famous rascal from this point of view. What you focus on, however, is his relation to the Peasant Wars, a relation which, as the plot develops, follows a twisting and contradictory course. Now, Marx called the Wars the 'most radical fact of German history'; bearing in mind that today we can call the establishment of a socialist society on German soil the 'most radical fact of German history', we gain some idea of the fundamental ties between the two ages.*

It is indeed the case that the character of Till Eulenspiegel can be set in various ages. Brecht, for instance, had the idea of setting an elderly Eulenspiegel in the period after the Peasant Wars, as a figure gathering together the downtrodden and the despairing and giving them encouragement. You could also see him as a timeless figure – the fool, in terms of both his role and function, in the Great Machine of History .... Right from the outset, we were interested in a character who, by dint of his experience of life, started out naive and credulous, and ended up seeing right through the power relations and conventions of his day, and at length – thoroughly without illusions, but by no means resigned to his fate – acquired the ability to cope with, indeed manipulate them. A forerunner, in other words, but not a revolutionary. As Friedrich Engels says when writing about the Peasant Wars: 'Before existing social relations could even be called into question, they had to be divested of their holy aura.' And debunking is exactly the job of the fool. The pillars of authority at the time – the Church, the feudal order, guilds etc. – had begun to totter, giving the outsider (for the fool is an outsider) ample scope for adventure. And we did not, by the way, seek to be faithful to history in a pernickety manner, for both the Eulenspiegel character and his circumstances contain elements of legend ....

I would be bored if the historical material I was working on did not have some relation to the present. As soon as we looked at Eulenspiegel, we realised that here was a man who meant something to us. I imagined a face that became harder yet more human as generations passed; I could imagine the attitudes of a man who, under great pressure, learned with supreme skill how best to use the means at his disposal, not simply in order to defend himself, but to extend the scope of real freedom both for himself and for the other commoners like him. We were attracted to this folk hero, this intelligent, cunning chap who dares to walk the tightrope. Moreover, the Renaissance is the age that gave birth to modern humanity; in it we find certain attitudes we immediately understand and with which we can empathise. It is also, however, an age we can keep at arm's length; our view of it is not prejudiced by direct involvement in the events of the time. What we have, in other words, is a kind of distanciation (*Verfremdung*), which permits us to deal with certain problems and conflicts which, for a variety of reasons, we do not or cannot yet say have concrete historical pertinence for the present. This is because the most radical fact of German history, i.e., the redirecting of society towards socialism from the roots up, does not always match the radicalism of our (historical, economic, socio-logical, moral and artistic) questioning of this society. But now we're get-ting into very big questions . . .

Hans Kaufmann: *Is it just coincidence, or is it, as I suspect, in the logic of your subject-matter, that there is more of the traditional epic in the plot of the film-script, than you recommend in your essay on 'The Reader and the Writer'? In your version, Eulenspiegel often gets involved in the struggles of the rising peasant and plebeian movement of the early sixteenth century. He is shaped by his actions and his sufferings; his experiences change and develop him. A causal connection is established between the various events; even the famous tricks he gets up to, some of which you include, acquire meaning only in the light of other episodes. In short, it is illuminating that the structure of character and plot that is produced by combining Eulen-spiegel with an emerging revolutionary movement is quite different from the one we find in the traditional folk tale. But doesn't that structure contradict the theory you expounded in 'The Reader and the Writer', which holds that the 'traditional', epic fable corresponds to a mechanistic view of the world? Precisely by trying to arrive at a dialectic of individuality and historical movement, don't you in fact end up here with an epic fable? I realise, of course, that a film script is not a piece of prose writing. And yet your argument confronts the relationship between world-view and struc-ture in such a general manner that it is impossible, taking the theory as it stands, to see why it should not also apply to film scripts. Or would you explain the difference by saying that the subject is set in a distant epoch that has come to an end, and that it is easier to see what that period led to than it is to survey the present? Is it to do with the fact that in this case you do not have to conceive or perceive yourself as an element in the action, so that ways of knowing and objectifying do not become problematic? If this were the case, Eulenspiegel woud lead us back to the questions we have already been discussing.*

I could choose to get out of this one easily by saying that 'The Reader and the Writer' you find me arguing that prose – at least, prose as I imagine it – is impossible to film. And in actual fact, this 'short story for a film' did emerge from a genuine scenario, and is in that sense not prose, which expresses precisely those invisible aspects of reality that the camera cannot capture. But this doesn't mean that historical dialectics can't be captured in a story, and I've never claimed otherwise. Leaving aside the obvious need, where any film is concerned, to make the development of the cast of characters visible, it's true that specific creative methods might be necessary when we take a step back into history, into a time about which we need to convey information. But as you've indicated, the main thing is that film necessarily lacks the fourth dimension of modern prose – what I call the dimension of the author, which I've described here as subjective authenticity. (This also gives me the chance to point out that personal *engagement* is not, and does not have to be, any less great where this kind of historical material is concerned.) I can't yet tell whether my current preoccupations with prose represent a transitional phase or whether they indicate any particular difficulties concerning knowledge and objectivity. At any rate it's unlikely that I'll 'change tack' in the future to forms of – how can I put it – conventional writing (though I don't like using perjorative terms), for these forms are now quite alien to me.

Above all, however, this film scenario's fourth dimension is left to the director and the actors. They have to be given scope to adopt their own approach to the substance of the work. And here lies the difference between writing for a film and writing a prose text. The same material would look quite different in prose form – though it wouldn't really be the 'same' material, of course.

Hans Kaufmann: *From the point of view of material, your short story* 'Selbstversuch' *('Self-Experiment'), which appeared in* Sinn and Form *in 1973, is 'hyper-modern', one might say, for the action presupposes that medical science can turn a woman into a man. How did you hit upon the idea?*

You're going to find this funny: 'Selbstversuch' was commissioned. One day Edith Anderson came up with the idea of producing an anthology. Five female and five male writers would each do a piece on the topic of 'When I was a man/woman'. I liked the thing, even though I cursed it a few times when I was actually writing. You see, the subject offered an opportunity for utopian mimicry – I like reading utopian books anyway, I just wish most of them were better! I immediately thought of a scientist who would be forced to help transform her own body for the sake of scientific progress. I am, in any case, interested in psychology, medicine, and the collective work of teams of scientists. I knew a thing or two about it, and could find out whatever else I needed to. But finding the right imaginative vehicle for this, putting the flesh on the bones of the idea, getting round the treatise-like nature of the question – that was difficult, and it remains problematic. I tried to make my job easier by highlighting the difficulties. The form, and indeed the whole thing, has an ironic feel to it: a report about a piece of scientific work that increasingly acquires the character of a subjective confession . . . .

Hans Kaufmann: *The story uses some of the paraphernalia of utopian science, though it only uses a little because you're clearly not concerned with expressing a utopian vision. The science fiction elements are, rather, merely instruments for analyzing a very contemporary problem: relations between the sexes. If I have understood correctly, your findings are not very encouraging. Humans are creating a more and more significant material built environment, and have even managed to change their biological nature, but they have neglected to change their social and human nature. This is brought out in relations between the sexes, the norms of which are still dictated by men and, as you rather clearly point out, uncritically accepted by women who interiorize those norms. 'Selbstversuch' ('Self-Experiment') was published along with Günter de Bruyn's 'Geschlechter-tausch' ('Changing Sex'), which takes a similar line. There is probably no fundamental difference between you, in terms of your theoretical appraisal of the problem, but there is in the execution a difference in emotional quality. De Bruyn largely treats the subject with a sense of satire and comedy – at times his tone is downright comic, though this is not to say he doesn't take the issue seriously. You, by contrast, betray unmistakable unease, even bitterness. Leaving aside the inevitable stylistic differences between two writers, could one conclude that she is less inclined to joke about this matter than he is?*

I'll have to keep a tight rein on myself here. We're getting on to one of those subjects where my blood tends to boil, because the danger is that our radical starting-point – the emancipation of women – gets obscured by our complacency about having battled our way through to what are really only preliminary stages, whereas in fact what we need are new radical ways of posing questions that can advance us further. The kind of questions I attempted to provoke through my story, might be: should the aim of women's emancipation be for them to 'become like men'?; would it even be desirable if they could do the same things, enjoy the same rights, so that men themselves would soon badly need emancipating?

I have deliberately tried this story out on the audience at many readings and watched for their reactions, especially their non-verbal reactions. Women laughing incredulously; young girls giggling as if you were telling them a dirty joke; men's down-turned mouths and stiff shoulders. Then suddenly their expressions – both men's and women's – change, they get agitated, they make excited gestures as they try and formulate their own experiences. How earnestly they grasp the opportunity to question a set of circumstances they had previously taken for granted. As the material conditions allowing the sexes an equal start improve – and this must necessarily be the first step towards emancipation – so we face more acutely the problem of giving the sexes opportunity to be different from each other, to acknowledge that they have different needs, and that men and women, not just men, are the models for human beings. This doesn't even occur to most men, and really very few women try and get to the root of why it is that their consciences are permanently troubled (because they can't do what's expected of them). If they got to the bottom of it, they'd find it was their own identification with an idealised masculinity that is in itself obsolete.

There you are, I've lost my sense of humour again. Although in fact my story does have a comic side to it, if you can call it comic, for the woman transforms herself into a man for the sake of the man she loves .... It's simply a matter of overcoming alienation, no more, no less. And we should be careful not to think we've already done that. I do feel we should pay more attention to such things as the use of scientific research, which is also questioned in the story, or to certain types of positivist thought that barricade themselves in behind so-called natural scientific method and ignore the human aspects. There is an interesting debate going on among scientists about these things; the very fact that they are being debated means I feel no need to be bitter about them.

It would also be worth considering whether, in a society which differs from bourgeois society in that it has a genuine sense of historical perspective, utopian features to some degree lend literature greater validity and perhaps even a sharper focus. This would simply mean that our society was in a position to render its own contradictions productive, and regard the conflicts that authors create as tools which can be usefully employed. That too is a process, of course.

Hans Kaufmann: 'Selbstversuch' *will also be included in the forthcoming volume subtitled* Drei unwahrscheinliche Geschichten *(Three Improbable Tales). The first of these,* 'Unter den Linden', *which also gives the book its title, relates a fictitious dream; the second the observations of a tom-cat, of all things; and the third we've already discussed. Apart from the 'improbability' of the stories, what the three pieces also have in common is that in them the unreal becomes a vehicle for analysing current problems. At the same time, there are differences between them, in terms not only of subject-matter but also of emotional tone.* 'Unter den Linden' *might be seen as expressing the inner struggle between depression and a new surge of enthusiasm for life; the* 'New View on Life of a Tom-Cat' *is a biting satire drawing on caricature and the grotesque. All three stories debate problems from contemporary life, and make out a case for change. Both their themes and the unusual way in which those themes are treated somehow challenge the reader. Now, I know that we literary critics like to categorize and classify, but are you embarking on a new phase in your work?*

I wrote the three stories between 1969 and 1972, and they are representative of that phase of my work (I was also writing other things, and had
started the larger project). It is not a coincidence that two of them are
deeply satirical, nor that I come up with one or two provocative
arguments. I hope that their 'improbability', their dreamlike, utopian and
grotesque character will produce an alienation-effect towards certain
processes, circumstances and modes of thought which have become so
very familiar that we no longer notice them, are no longer disturbed by
them. And yet we should be disturbed by them – and I say this in the
confident belief that we can change what disturbs us.

  A 'new' phase? No, I don't think so. Little experiments with new tools,
perhaps, testing out methods that appeal to me. Whether I'll use them
again later, I can't tell.

Hans Kaufmann: *You've aready hinted at an answer to the question a journalist would be bound to ask you – what are you working on at the
moment? I would like to slant the other inevitable question, about your
plans for the future, in a more problematizing, more provocative way, if you
like. Since 'The Divided Heaven', the image of the writer Christa Wolf has
been based in considerable measure on the seriousness you bring to the
great moral questions of our time. This has continued through* Christa T. *to
the* Improbable Tales. *The advancement of socialism demands that human-
ist principles of behaviour take firm root within human beings, and become
the subjective motives behind their actions. Such an attitude serves as the
necessary starting point for fictions which communicate socialist-humanist
impulses. This for me is beyond all doubt, even though I should perhaps
add that the problem of humanism is here posed in a one-sided fashion –
merely theoretically, as a matter of thought and feeling alone. Artistic activity can 'sublate' [aufheben] this one-sidedness by bringing it to consciousness. Satire, for instance, implies one-sidedness, imbalance; reading a work
as a satire means mentally 'redressing' the imbalances portrayed. Something similar holds for works such as your* Improbable Tales, *that are based
on the unreal and the fantastic. So far, so good. But we can't overlook the
fact that the establishment of humanism is not only a matter of thought and
feeling, but also – or rather primarily – of practical, material, social activity. If 'making humans human' is seen merely as having to do with the
acquisition of moral values and not also (perhaps even primarily) as the
bringing to fruition of skills, capacities and dispositions, does this not rather
limit the possibilities of art's impact (just to take one aspect of the question)? Is there not a danger that a human being's thoughts and actions
might be regarded as being opposed to one another, rather than being seen
as standing in a vital contradiction whose inner unity and motion distinguishes the 'whole person'? To get back to my original question about*

your future plans, do these or similar considerations play a part in your thinking? Might they affect what you choose to write about in the future, and how you will tackle your subject matter?

I'm afraid I haven't perhaps grasped your meaning, because I don't see such a gulf between the 'acquisition of moral values' and the way in which humans become human through their active involvement in the process of historical change.

Hans Kaufmann: *My question – and it is a question, not a demand – concerns whether in the future you as a writer will be interested in those changes in the human psyche that are engendered by practical activity.*

You mean, whether I would find the subject of material production interesting?

Hans Kaufmann: *That would be one example, yes.*

I might cite, 'The Divided Heaven', though I realise you may think it belongs too much in the past to be relevant to your question. But even there I was of course interested not only in material production – material production in the sense of the labour process itself, operating mechanical equipment, the endlessly repetitive motions of a production line, being shackled to the instrument panel of a machine. The only kind of 'praxis' that literature can use creatively is social praxis. The relationships that producers establish with each other and with other institutions and social strata as they go about their production; how and to what extent – I must come back to this – their practical activity enables them to take part in the historical process of change: these are the interesting points. This is, of course, an enormous subject, and it is one that I may possibly come back to dealing with directly.

On the other hand I don't think my work has ever appealed to an abstract morality, to an authority soaring above the raging sea of the class struggle from which a socialist author could take guidance.

Hans Kaufmann: *I wasn't implying that either.*

I reject moral voyeurism by any author, and this is a major reason why I attempt to write in a certain fashion. I insist writers should expose themselves to contradictions . . .

At the same time I don't share the contempt some Marxists show for the little word 'morality', for the very reason I have already mentioned. I cannot, will not be swayed by the kind of crude historical determinism that regards individuals, groups, class and peoples as nothing but the objects of relentless laws of historical development, and which amounts to a fatalistic philosophy of history. Nor will I be convinced by any soulless pragmatism that sees the morality of classes and individuals as nothing but a means to an end to be manipulated or ignored at will, as a vehicle to be used or discarded as they wish. Which of us is not touched by the pain and tragedy of Brecht's words: 'We who wished to lay the ground for friendliness, could not ourselves be friendly'?

'How must the world be constituted for a moral being?' Bobrowski's question is still provocative, for it urges that the world be adapted to a morality of human dignity, not that human morality be adapted to a world that still abuses human dignity. To do the latter would be to invite the physical death of humanity . . . .

None of this has anything to do with Christian antinomies of good and evil, with a rigid contradistinction between thought and deed, nor with an abstract, fruitless and ultimately paralyzing demand for integrity. Indeed, our errors can be 'moral' if they continually allow us productively to resolve our contradictions. By contrast, everything that prevents us, that prevents the masses from becoming the subject rather than the object of history, is immoral. So, proceeding from this argument, why can't socialist writers be 'moralists' too?

My feeling is that the issues that arise within this whole area of problems, including the potential it contains for personal conflict, provide more than enough material for the things I would still like to write: indeed, they could keep literature busy for an age. I do have short-term and long-term plans, but it's much too early to talk about them.

1973

3

A MODEL OF EXPERIENCE

A Discussion on *A Model Childhood**

Question: *I would be interested to know what prompted you to write this kind of book. Were you commissioned to write it or was it your own idea?*

It is surely obvious when you read the book that it could not have been written in response to an external commission. I had always planned to write something like this, ever since I began writing. Not exactly this, of course, but something that covers my own lifetime, or at least tries to get nearer to it. Even now I have written it, I still find it very difficult to explain. Still, I could say something a little more precise about what inspired me to write the book. It is expressed in the chapter we are discussing in the words of a Polish writer whose thoughts correspond to my own. Like him, I have the impression that despite having read, heard and in some cases written an enormous amount about the fascist period in Germany, we basically still know very little about it. The question, 'How was it possible, and what was it really like?' remains in principle unanswered. I am well aware, of course, that this can't be rectified in a book like this. I'm certainly not so arrogant as to think that.

But I do think that those who lived through this period and who know how powerfully, how far and in what ways it moulded them as people, have a certain duty to put this into words. As far as they are able. That is what prompted me to write the book.

It disturbs me a little that many of our books on this period end with heroes experiencing a kind of instant metamorphosis and, even under fascism, managing to arrive at important, correct ideas on both the

*This text, which was originally published in *Sinn und Form*, no. 4, 1976, is an edited version of the discussion which followed a reading from *A Model Childhood* at the GDR Academy of Arts on 8 October and 3 December 1975.

political and human level. I don't want to dispute the personal experience of any author, but my own experience was very different. I found that it was a very long time before I gained even the first limited insights, and only later did more profound changes become possible.

I think all this has to be said. Whether it is still of interest to younger people who did not share out experience, I cannot say. Nor does this undermine what I have said. It is this sense of a lacuna, this feeling that something is missing, that inspires me to write, the feeling that readers in other countries should perhaps know about these things, that they want to learn what really went on inside people at that time.

Question: *Why did you choose this particular subject? Isn't it more important to write about the present?*

Do you think I'm not writing about the present? Look, as long as people whose childhood or youth was conditioned by the experience of these years are still alive, then it all remains inside them. They live with it. And I think – indeed, I am quite convinced – that there is much all of us have not yet said about this period either to ourselves or to others. For years I felt very keenly that I myself hadn't yet managed to do this and it was something I had to do if I was to go on to write other things. Certain laws of professional morality come into play here. There are some things which have to be said before you can pass on to others.

I have said this many times before, but I will say it again here: in my experience, people of my own age – I see that most of you here today are younger, much younger than I am – but people of my age, that is the parents of many of you here, talk very little about this period either amongst themselves or with their children, and never openly. This is one of the reasons why I wanted to write this book. I think this has to be included in what we call the 'present'. To see the present as only what happens today would be to assign the concept a very narrow meaning. The present is everything that today, for example, impels us to act or not act, determines how we act or choose not to.

Question: *You said that morally and spiritually we have not yet got over the fascist past. I agree with you completely. And you say far too little has been done to determine how the younger generation, born too late to experience this period themselves, can be given a realistic picture of it. I can only agree with you there too, and I admire you greatly for having dared to take steps to remedy the situation. Nevertheless, one thing concerns me. I fear that because of the essayistic form and the rather complex presentation of the period, only those sections of the reading public who view these kinds of things on a more intellectual plane will be reached. I'm not advocating some kind of primitivism, but I'd be interested to know why you have moved away, by comparison with your first novel for example, from the traditional form of the novel with its action and plot, which, I think, reaches a wider audience?*

I understand your question, of course. It is something I am frequently asked. But how am I to answer?

Question: *What I'm trying to say is that there are always people who think that they are particularly clever and that others are very stupid. They tend to feel that even though they can understand something, others unfortunately won't be able to. They usually mean the 'ordinary person' (in inverted commas) will not understand it. They therefore conclude that artists must apply themselves to what the ordinary person can understand. I think this is a great fallacy. And if the people here in this room understand your work, then that is enough. One shouldn't go round thinking all the time that others are more stupid than oneself.*

Thank you. I know you didn't mean the question like that. But you know, the first reaction to everything I write is, 'But it's so difficult!' You couldn't know this, but I still remember that it was just the same with 'The Divided Heaven' – 'So difficult!' But if you read it today, the idea seems ridiculous.

Question: *Perhaps that's because you have read it often enough?*

I have never re-read it. But there is no point in me evading the question, as I don't hold with artificially complicating a matter with no regard to how many people will be left who can follow my chain of thought. That is not what I think writing is about at all. On the contrary, I think one should make it as simple as possible. But then with some subjects there is a problem: how simple can it be made?

I often start over and over again. I spent more than a year on this manuscript before I even had a beginning. I abandoned a great number of pages where I had experimented with different narrative forms, none of which satisfied me. You don't know exactly what you want when you're writing. You just have a kind of narrative tone in your ear and an atmosphere, something like that .... And a narrative space you'd like to fill. And then you begin to write, in a linear fashion, for example. In this case, this seemed a bit 'thin' to me, 'thin' in the sense that it did not fill the whole space. It created a narrative line, but not a space. And only gradually – it took a very long time – did I realize that I would have to include in the text how the manuscript itself emerged, which I did with some reluctance.

And reflections on memory too: what exactly is this process of remembering, what does one remember, why does one remember some things and
not others? It then became part of the project to discuss the concept of
remembering as well. And so there gradually developed three or four of
these 'planes', including the journey to Poland described throughout this
chapter, because it was important to me to show what it is like to arrive in
a town which is now Polish but which is also one's home town. That is an
experience common to many of us that has until now hardly been articulated and which needed time, I think, these last few decades, before it
could be articulated. Homesickness has been an important factor. It was
through these various levels and the way they combined that I first
realized this could become a book about the present.

This explains the structure of the book. After that, I could no longer
make the basic structure simpler.

Question: *I am delighted that you try to present the past in a way which
allows us to identify with it and that you connect it with our present.
Especially for younger people this opens up the way towards understanding, presenting the problems as though they were contemporary. In the
same way you manage to keep a certain sense of detachment from our
generation so that people can relive their own experience but are no longer
over-involved in it. I am delighted I was able to hear your reading.*

Thank you. You know, if you ask what literature can achieve today, a
great variety of responses can be given, most of them 'correct'. They will
differ from author to author, and that is, I think, only right and proper. I
came to literature, or rather experienced a compulsion to write, from
having been – and still being – very powerfully and very personally
affected by history, by the history of our people, our state and all the
events I have consciously experienced since childhood. It seems to me that
it is essential and that it could be of general use, apart from being useful to
me, to try to set in motion again the hidden layers and deposits that these
events have left buried in us all. I know opinion varies on this, doesn't it?
One view of course is that we should leave well alone – it's not helpful, it's
disturbing, we can do without that right now. It is an old argument and
one we will probably hear again and again, each time something new
crops up.

My opinion is that literature ought to try to reveal these layers buried
inside us; they are not so neatly and tidily organized, not so catalogued
and nicely 'dealt with', as we like to think. I don't think that we have
'dealt with' the fascist period in this sense, even if we have set about this in
an incomparably different and more fundamental way than has been the
case, for example, in the Federal Republic. I am speaking here of a different

kind of 'dealing with' things: the way individuals analyze their own past, what they personally did and thought, matters on which they cannot pass the buck, things which cannot simply be excused on the grounds that masses of people did the same or worse. Here, sociology and statistics cannot help us. This is a question of personal and social morality and the conditions that cause both to break down.

In this sense we have not 'dealt' with it. I see this in the questions that young people ask, and I see it in the silence of my contemporaries and older people. Only literature can tackle these questions, this silence. I am not criticizing other forms of expression – the journalistic report or the historical account for instance. They don't do this, because it isn't their job. I think it is up to literature to stir these inner layers into some kind of motion. Their present immobility in fact only brings us peace of mind because we take what is in reality merely mental paralysis for that true peace of mind which can only come from inner freeedom. Here though, as you correctly recognized, the present is the motor, the constant driving force. I didn't know either, of course, when I began to write the manu-script three or four years ago, that in 1973 events in Chile would upset us all so much. One cannot foresee these things.

Question: *This kind of topic demands such great poise in approaching the present and the past. When you were working on it, did you feel you were in the right place to enable you to write about it?*

I must say that whilst I was writing – although every possible emotion, including 'negative' and even depressing ones, was of course strongly associated with it – I still felt that I was in the right place. This is because trying to get one's own experience clear in one's own mind is not merely a meditative process. I would not have wanted therefore to cut myself off on some remote island. Here, where everything around me affects me, is the right place for me to remember. 'Action' is a vast concept. I know what you're driving at. You are suggesting that none of us could have prevented what has just happened in Spain for example,* that we cannot stop this or that happening in our own country, let alone the world. Nevertheless, I feel that consciousness is growing, not just the purely political, ideological consciousness which we take as our fundamental starting point, but consciousness in the sense in which I mean it too. There has also been an increase in the consciousness of our own role in the historical process. Hence an increase in activity, activity which also expresses itself in a growing need to communicate with others and to unite with them. Just as we are doing this evening. This is a new atmosphere. That, at least, is my

*The reference is to the execution of five Spanish anti-fascists on 27 September 1975 – Tr.

impression, I think this is a good place for all this for all sorts of reasons, including, among others, geographical reasons. I think this is a good spot for getting a clear view of what is happening in the world and the way things are moving.

Question: *How do you want the novel to end? At what stage do you want it to break off?*

I can give you a definite answer to that. I have said there will be eighteen chapters. It was never my intention to write a novel about the metamorphosis of a person, nor would it suit the style I chose. So I don't follow this person referred to as Nelly far into the post-war period, but only into the very first year after the war, into the confusion that is left. Her home town is evacuated, and people begin to flee. I don't think this process has been described before, perhaps because the young men had not returned from the war then and not many women write. Perhaps few writers experienced this exodus, this nomadic existence on the streets. And then, after May 1945, the first contact with people from another world, with a Jewish officer in the American occupying forces or with a concentration camp prisoner. And that goes on into the first part of 1946. What happens after that is mentioned briefly. What does happen, by the way, is complete turmoil and it is this that stimulated me to write because the way the immediate post-war years are often described does not bear any relation to my own experience. My own experience was completely different and this too encouraged me to try and write about it. Perhaps today, after thirty years, this is possible, perhaps not. I have attempted it anyway. Of course, this strand of the plot, which is carried along by the future of Nelly and runs far into 1946, increasingly comes up against questions from the present.

Question: *Since your book concerns the problem of youth and childhood under Nazism, did it ever perhaps occur to you to write this book in the first person, that is from Nelly's point of view? To take this girl as the subjective 'I', to get inside her, for example in the scene at the sports tournament, which you describe rather from the point of view of the adults: crowds of people, strain, sweat, flags covered in swastikas. I don't know if you were there or not. But might you not have described that directly from the little girl's point of view, in terms of the emotions it evoked for her?*

Yes, of course, I considered that. I said earlier that I made several different beginnings, and most of these were in the first person. For reasons which weren't clear to me then and which I didn't really understand properly, it was this which always proved to be an obstacle to really getting to grips with the subject. Now of course, I understand quite well the reasons for this. And other things then came to me too – I don't think that I ever hide the fact that the book is, so to speak, autobiographical. I admit this. But this 'so to speak' is very important because I do not feel identity with my character. There is, and this is perhaps one of the peculiarities of my life story, though others of my age may have the same experience, a sense of alienation from this period. From a definite moment, which one cannot trace to the exact day but certainly to the exact period, one is no longer the same person. I no longer feel that it was I who had thought, said or done those things. And that's what I wanted to express through the third person, or rather had to, because otherwise the material remained closed to me, as I learned from my various attempts to make a start.

Somebody asked how the book ends. It ends with the voices of the third person, Nelly, and the second person which is also in there, coming together and forming a single person, the 'I', which must then be narrated in a different way: different in content and different in form.

But it wasn't only a need to find an alternative to the 'I' in the third person, which I don't deny, but above all an uncanny feeling of alienation. As if I would be deceiving both myself and the reader if I called this being 'I' ... And it was exactly this feeling which I wanted to express by using the third person, because another result of this often disrupted life story is that several people wander around inside our bodies, and it is not at all easy to work out how to relate to all of them. This is the real reason the person was split into the familiar '*Du*' and the formal '*Sie*' forms.

Question: *I don't think the book is only of interest to older people. I was amazed by this mixture of, let us say, essay writing and poetry and, above all, by the intensity and the turn to science and to psychology. I think this is something new, which will also appeal to young people. My question is, are you modelling yourself on someone here or how did you come to give this question such emphasis? This is something I have only seen previously in Granin's work. How did this development come about in your own writing?*

I find this a bit embarrassing. It is of course stupid to say that one has no models for one's writing, because naturally one has not completely invented it oneself. But if I say Musil, for example, did something along the same lines, then it sounds as if I took Musil as my model. But this isn't true, although I find Musil a very interesting author – one of many. But I feel this style emerged from a certain necessity. I spent a long time looking for it. I don't think that I will always write this way. I already have a few stories in mind which will contain only a small reflective element, or none at all, because, in my opinion, they don't need it.

Question: *What interests me are your various experiments with the telling of this story. Are these experiments conducted from the author's point of view, to establish how one can best get to grips with the narrative, or from the point of view of the group it is aimed at: 'How can I explain this to my child today?'*

I sense that a lot of younger people, particularly those born between 1935 and 1945, that is those born during the war years, but who hardly remember the war at all now, really don't want to know anything more about it. They bury their heads in the sand . . . . I know this from my own family. I don't know how representative this is or to what extent it has been studied. I can imagine, though, that it is the different levels, for example the reference to Chile, that will appeal more to such people, precisely because it is a book that deals with the present as well as events from the past. Is one justified in saying this?

To answer your first question: it seems strange for a biologist to be asking about the meaning of experiments. Of course these are not done with the target audience in mind. It is, in any case, a misconception that one has the reader in mind as one writes. I'm certainly not one of those writers who claim that they never think about the fact that at some point what they write will be published, and I don't believe writers who do. It's not true. You don't think about it, but you are aware of it, it is there. You would like your writing to be published, you write it for publication. To that extent, writing is different from making notes in your diary about childhood or something. That is the first thing.

I was not concerned with any potential reader while I was experimenting, but with the subject matter, the material. It was a kind of self-experiment. One has to achieve some kind of relation to one's material, and this is what I was trying to do. I could see what was there in front of me and how it must necessarily unfold, but at that stage I had no relation to it. The point of the experiments was to create that relation. You see this when you start off speaking and have the right tone, and you find you can listen to yourself and believe what you are saying. At some point, you might lose that tone and have to search for it again. That is the effort writing demands if it is not to become a merely routine process.

On your second point, about younger people, it is really difficult for me to answer. I don't know myself whether these particular people you have in mind are, or wish to be, especially ignorant about this period. It is possible that school has inoculated them against a properly questioning attitude to it. This could be the case. I have looked at our history books, especially on this era, and have found, thank God – this is really a great step forward – that there is nothing in them that is untrue. They state what really happened. On the other hand I know from young people that they treat this like they do anything else, and teachers, who may well be the same age as me, cannot make them react to this subject emotionally with any more involvement than they show towards anything else. Take the map in the fourth-year history textbook, for example, where all the concentration camps are marked. I have seen young people of thirteen and fourteen in Buchenwald walk across what used to be the rollcall square, munching away, radios blaring. Something hasn't been awakened in them – I'm not talking about a sense of guilt, but a sense of sympathy. This gives me pause for thought. This map of the concentration camps is there in the books and is truthfully represented. And yet it seems to me it produces no more emotion than any other map in the book.

Yes, it's true. I would like to make it harder to forget. One can of course condemn this, and I know that many people will condemn it with the old saying: just when we've buried all the old dirt, along comes some young whipper-snapper and rakes it all up again. But that is exactly my function. I am the young whipper-snapper here raking it all up again – quite deliberately. That is what I would like to do, what I want to do. Whether or not it is what others will want now was something I couldn't ask while I was writing.

Question: *You say that sympathy denied to our generation in its childhood turns to fear later, that one becomes concerned only about one's material existence, that one can no longer show solidarity with people .... Is that your concern, the gradual elimination of the fear we acquired then? A fear which leads us to forget? A fear which suppresses any ability to talk to young people so that they are moved emotionally and see that it wasn't just a joke when Adolf Hitler spoke to us, but that something had been set free which took hold of us. Is writing your way of trying to overcome this fear, and what means do you suggest to other people who do not have the possibility of writing open to them to break down this fear?*

You have grasped what I was trying to do extraordinarily well. That is exactly how it is. For me it is a way to overcome fear. Or, if it cannot be overcome, then at least to make myself conscious of it, and be able to live with it, without letting it restrict me.

I would like to be a little more specific, since how fear emerges is a central problem of this book. Right at the end, there is a chapter that will be entitled 'A Chapter of Fear', and it will stir up again and bring together all those fears of the most horrendous kind that were built up inside us. The fear of other peoples for example. 'The Russian' as figure of fear, how is that possible, how was it created, in what ways should such real fears be dismantled? One loses the fear of individuals, peoples, groups when one gets to know them. This is a relatively – and I stress relatively – simple psychological process. You can unlearn false images, images of fear, by replacing them with correct ones. For the human race today, moulded by distorted images of fear, this is an important – perhaps life-saving – process.

It is different, on the other hand, with apparently groundless fear which I believe many people are stricken with from time to time. Here it is much more difficult to trace the origin of the fear and ascertain why it lasts so long, and quite specific symbols arouse fear again and again. Why, for example, many people of our generation have such a terrible fear of authority. When was this injected into them? Why can so many people in our country only stand up for themselves against authority in fear? Why do they find it so difficult to 'cock a snook' at little kings and princes? There are reasons for this. This is why I see my book as a book about the present, because it tries to describe what led up to people behaving the way they do today.

Yes, I too see those who write or paint, or practice any other art, as being at an advantage, because they have an effective opportunity to analyze conflicts. But I think really that anyone can do this if they really want and need to, either by themselves or by talking to other people. But why, oh why, do we talk to each other so little? From fear of course. But fear of what, for God's sake? Certainly not usually a fear of someone hurting us. It's fear of ourselves, a fear that we might let something slip which other people won't forget, and that they would then have us in the palm of their hands. It would be better if they would forget it, but they never forget, so we prefer not to say anything in the first place. So we sit and talk about the weather and pass on gossip and never ever talk – I suppose I'm exaggerating: a lot of people, I hope, have people with whom they talk – but, I think, many people never talk about what is really worrying them and I think that is awful.

Question: *I have great expectations of your novel. It deals with the experiences of my parents and above all evaluates their experiences under fascism. I hope to be able to understand certain things better, including things which have a bearing on my own childhood and youth as well.*

I do understand what you mean. But I find this kind of attitude of expectation a little oppressive almost. A book can't solve all our problems, and neither can I, of course.

I know I won't be able to fulfil all the expectations. And, you know, something I didn't know before but came to realize as I wrote the book, is that childhood is an incredibly intimate experience, and I'm not absolutely positive that I would have embarked on the book had I known this earlier. It contains so much that one is ashamed of, all kinds of things which one doesn't talk about. I think that it is partly generationally specific too, so the model childhood of your generation can only really be described by people of your own age. What there is in my book about your generation, and I hope there will be something about it, is, of course, a reflection of my own relation to it. But I don't really get inside you. I got deep inside myself, though I can scarcely believe that I did. But I can't get inside the twenty-year-olds of today. I try to observe them very carefully, with interest and commitment, but, nonetheless, I know for certain that I'm not inside their world.

So I very much hope that when you are twenty-five, thirty or even older, one of you will write this for your generation. It's a subject that can't be delegated to anyone else. But you are absoluely right, I hope that people of your age will find something of relevance to them in the book, perhaps in the sense you suggest. I don't know, I can only hope.

Question: *I think that the fears you have just expressed are somewhat exaggerated. I think by analyzing these problems, which we haven't fully come to terms with yet, and by analyzing them really honestly and intensively, we may actually speed up the 'biological process' for the young people of today. You said at the beginning, when asked why you couldn't devote yourself to current issues, that for you this is a current issue. I think that the subject you address is just as topical today, because you are reflecting it from the present day. In this respect, I think that it is important that you remain honest with yourself, even at the risk of putting off some readers. In return, those who do read the book will do so more intensively, and get more out of it in the end. I think this is very valuable, and feel that generally the important thing is to express oneself honestly, not to confine oneself within certain set lines of development.*

Yes, that is certainly true. You are right, one should try to do this. And I'm not saying I don't think young people will find something in the book – I would be being over-modest, even dishonest, if I suggested that I sincerely hope they will find something in it. What I meant earlier was that we must simply accept that the truth is concrete, and that the concrete truth of your youth is diferent from the concrete truth of mine. There can be patterns of childhood which are generally applicable to all generations in their youth, or to a specific century, country or society. In this sense, I hope people will find some things of general validity in the book.

To continue on the subject of honesty. I perhaps aroused too many hopes there too. Just yesterday, in the chapter I am currently working on, I wrote that it is an illusion to think one can be honest. I don't want to spread this illusion. I had already realized this earlier, but now I saw quite specifically that one never quite succeeds in being completely honest. For many reasons, most of which can be laid at one's own door. I have no intention of pushing the blame on to some external force, and certainly not on to some social determinant that might somehow prevent us from being honest. I think we should have learned that this isn't what is really important. What is really important is what one can achieve oneself, with regard to oneself. And one can only achieve this approximately. And this holds true for this book. I know that now and I have to accept it.

Question: *This book will stir back into life a whole swathe of the past for our generation, the generation that now occupies the positions of responsibility in the economy, politics, art and education. Generally attitudes only become more authoritarian than they already are because there doesn't seem to be any time for debate. It would be a great achievement if our generation were compelled, by reading your book, into reflections of this kind.*

You know, the people you have in mind probably won't read the book. Not out of any ill-will, they just don't have time to, their life passes literature by. But you are absolutely right, I have often found myself in the company of people of my age or thereabouts, a little older as well, who only need a few glasses of schnapps or wine to bring out a completely different side of their personality, to sing a quite different song from the one they have just been singing. I must admit this really annoys me – it really does – but at the same time, I can understand. For these are the consequences of never having thought about oneself, never having reflected, never having posed the question of one's own guilt. You can apportion that to the others: the 'better history' is on our side, the others are unlucky, they have the old Nazis. Certainly, I believe we can refer to our better tradition – and this, incidentally, is an enormous piece of luck for us and can be a source of great productivity – but only if everything else, including in our own lives, is not forgotten. That really does not help. But many prefer to repress the memories.

And this is why thirty-year-olds go to other socialist countries and sing hair-raising songs round the campfire – scenes like this happen here too, by the way. That was one of the reasons why I wrote the book. But, you know, you can't expect to achieve too much. Literature, I think, has very intense effects, but it achieves them in such a subterranean way that it is difficult to measure.

I've thought about all this a great deal. In 1945 when the war had just ended, I was just sixteen years old, and for a year or two, I devoured all the old books I could lay my hands on greedily and with great relish. I don't mean the Nazi books in the narrow sense of the word but the bland, meaningles stuff by Binding, and the novels of Carossa and Jelusich. This revealed the damage done to my whole perceptive apparatus. I couldn't see clearly. I couldn't see literature clearly, which all went to prove that I couldn't perceive reality clearly. Something had been seriously damaged.

And now to what we mean when we say a person 'changes'. To take up an earlier question, for me it basically comes down to repairing this perceptive apparatus that has been so seriously damaged and re-establishing the correct reactions to reality, so that one is able to live in reality, with reality, and in a way adapted to reality, that is, to act in a way that influences reality. None of this was ever possible. A whole generation, more than one, had suffered great damage to the fundamental principles of its psychic existence on earth. That cannot be so easily repaired. It is not suddenly the end of the problem if, two years later, you turn round and say, my God, Marx was right after all.

Question: *In your childhood did you come across people who talked critically of Adolf Hitler, Nazism and the final victory, or who told political jokes?*

Not one, not a single one! That's precisely the point. I never met one. And this is why I've always been a little dissatisfied (for all their merits) by the books published here in the GDR about this period. Not one of them reflected my experience. Usually what happened was that at some point or other, someone approached the young hero and said, 'Listen, son, you are really going wrong now.' And I thought I must have been a very exceptional case never to have had that happen to me, until, during the great postwar exodus which I also describe in my book, a concentration camp prisoner, sitting round the campfire with us, said: 'Where were you all?'

I didn't understand the question at all. It just stuck in my mind. It was only much much later that I finally understood it.

Question: *What made a deep impression on me in this chapter is that this schoolgirl, the BDM member,* * *despite having very different convictions, doesn't report the teacher. This is what makes this literature different even from that used in schools, which emphasises how critical people were in the fascist period. There is no mention of the inner emigration.† Everybody was somehow involved in resistance struggles against the Nazis, hiding Jews and Communists in spite of the danger to their own lives. At the end of the war I was five years old, and I'm not really guilty of anything. Nevertheless*

---

* *Bund Deutscher Mädchen*, the German Girls' League, which was the female counterpart of the Hitler Youth – Tr.

† A term usually applied to the withdrawal into private life of artists and intellectuals who remained in Germany throughout the Nazi period but did not support the Third Reich – Tr.

I've talked to people – classmates, schoolmates – of the same age, and we are in a very strange intermediate position between those before us and those after us, who were both fired with enthusiasm. I find the fact that those in my age group were not at all enthusiastic difficult. That might be a good thing, I suppose. It also leads to a sense of being ashamed to be German. I can't rid myself of this, especially when I'm abroad. Sometimes, when you are abroad, someone will suddenly address you in German and tell you that he was an interpreter during the war. He wants to show you that he bears no grudge against you. It is so dreadful to know that my father would have shot at him. I really just want to say that this kind of literature basically makes life a little easier because it talks about this experience.

What you said at the end about the problem of being a German is something I can relate to very cleary. And I'm going to say something now that will probably surprise you: I have completely lost this feeling. I no longer feel any sense of shame about being German. This occurred to me whilst you were talking and at the same moment I realized how it came about – it came from my contact with Soviet people, friends, who were all in the war, who were officers or who published newspapers for the front, and a Soviet professor of history, who sadly is dead now – this occurs in the book by the way – with whom I talked as much about Hitler as I did about Stalin. The first non-German people (in fact the first people at all) to whom I talked about this period and my experiences of it, were Soviet citizens. We also talked about the immediate post-war period and what the Soviet troops experienced. They were the first who wanted to hear about it, the first to say 'Write it down!'. I think my close relationship to these people gradually made me lose this sense of shame at being German. I no longer have it. But I understand it very well. I remember for instance how terribly psychologically draining my first trips to the Soviet Union were.

To turn briefly to the first part of the question. This girl does not report the music teacher. It is a 'real life' scene. The music teacher, having lost his son, insulted us and, by so doing, put himself in great danger. Today I realize just how much danger he put himself in, by saying, 'The Jewish girls have sung the Christian songs and you want to refuse to sing a Jewish Christmas carol?' And this girl, my friend, was a committed BDM leader but she didn't report him. It would never have occurred to her to report him, because at the same time she respected him as a music teacher and was one of his best pupils. It wasn't that simple. And that's what I would really like to try to do, temper some of these old clichés a bit.

Question: *If I understand you correctly, you are asking, 'What really did happen to us?', that is, 'How could such a thing happen?' Your book of*

*course is much much longer than the excerpt you read for us, but neverthe-
less these questions, 'What did happen to us?', 'How could such a thing
happen?' were not answered anywhere. Neither was the question – a question which troubles me even more than the first – 'Could it not happen
again?'*

I cannot say much about the first part of your question. I said at the begin-
ing that I don't pretend to be able to answer the question 'How could that
happen?' That I cannot say. Perhaps I could answer the question 'How did
we become the people that we are?' better. That is really the question
which I aim to come a little closer to answering. I think that the book will
shed a glimmer of light on this because I think part of what our generation
does or doesn't do today is connected with its childhood. If childhood
really is an important period in one's life, then we shouldn't act as if, at
sixteen years of age, with fascism at an end, we could suddenly become
'new people' and that such a misspent childhood would not leave its
mark.

But to come to your second question. Yes, I do think it would be
impossible for it to happen again here. As we can see, the world as a whole
is incredibly threatened by fascist and fascistic influences. The reasons
why it cannot happen here again, though, are, I think, first and foremost
historical. I don't want to set myself up as some kind of prophet, but the
necessary conditions do not exist here. As we have seen, though, these
conditions do exist in many parts of the world and they do not simply
make the outbreak of naked violence and brutality and its consolidation in
forms of State power possible, but they may also prolong such a situation
for a considerable time. These really are historically determined events.

Your question about the subjective factors involved is a different
matter. My manuscript contains indications of the fact that I am
constantly aware of the threat to individual people including people in the
GDR – sometimes it is just a matter of thoughtlessness, sometimes it is
more than that. Many things are involved: thoughtlessness, ignorance, a
sheltered existence. Then people, even here, can suddenly reveal horrifying
characteristics.

Question: *Does your material have to be taken from real life, and does the
actual writing process depend on a degree of detachment from specific
events?*

In this case I have taken almost thirty years to distance myself from the
events – I was twenty-five when I began. How great this detachment must
be, how many years are needed, depends on how deeply one was affected.
In this case the seriousness of the injury, the wound, which must be

expressed meant the question could not be broached earlier. This explains why I needed such a long time before I could embark on the book. In other cases the time may be much shorter. This was something which needed this amount of time. It varies.

Question: *You said that we haven't yet got over the past. But can we ever get over it? In actual fact, young people have had it right up to here, the past I mean. They read about it, they're interested in it, even though they weren't alive at the time. In fact it is the older people, for whom it perhaps has more direct significance, who don't show any interest in it at all. Most of them just don't talk about it.*

I often get the impression that this is the case. The older generation, those who are older than me, who basically should have considered this whole question of guilt in personal terms, have actually avoided it most, and it is these people whom it is most difficult to get to talk about it, perhaps even to think about it. We have no idea what they think. Our generation, which was too young to be guilty in any direct sense, in terms of what they actually did, has felt the whole burden of this guilt fall on them. I feel I'm justified in saying this. And those younger than us who now confront us as their parents or teachers and say, 'What went wrong then, what was it all about, what did you really see, do and think?' .... It is really rather complicated. and when you ask, 'Is it possible to get over it?', I can only say frankly, no it's not. Six million murdered Jews is not something you can come to terms with. That twenty million Soviet citizens were killed is not something you can 'get over'. All this is not something we can become reconciled to.

Question: *Is there any point writing about it, then?*

That is what I had to ask myself. I think there is a point to it. I don't just live for today, but for a tomorrow. It is quite possible that some readers think that there are already enough books on the subject and mine is superfluous. I can't make a judgement on that. But it would be presumptuous to think we could 'come to terms' with the matter through writing.

But, as I said earlier, the question of whether one should be constantly living with experiences that one would basically rather forget, whether there is any point in this, whether it contributes to one's productivity, is a different question and could be answered in various ways. In my experience, one needs to do this in order to be productive. There are dangers though, ones I am quite familiar with. Working on something like this releases a lot of things from one's past. The book contains many dreams, since working on this kind of material is naturally not conducive to pleasant dreams. Fears are released which you didn't even know were still there, fears which are still live fears now, and for the first time you understand why you are afraid of things in the present which ought to be quite harmless. But fear has become bound up with quite specific processes which are connected for example with authority. If you never get this clear in your own mind and never learn consciously to confront it in your life, then the fear will remain.

Question: *At the beginning, you said, or at least I undersood you to be saying, that your work is directed towards people of your own generation, who lived through the same things as you, and that you remained open-minded as to whether young people – i.e. those who didn't share these experiences – understand it in the same way. From what you have read for us today, one can infer that you are essentially trying, by association, to provide a reassessment of the memories of those who shared these experiences. The question I want to ask here is whether you believe that information, experience, really can be passed down from generation to generation. I ask this because, again and again, in all spheres of life, one sees young people striving eagerly to get closer to the past, to absorb information in quite a sophisticated way, and yet the past cannot really be appreciated if it is only absorbed intellectually. One can only understand something properly if it is reinforced in one associatively, if it has established itself as a memory, and is experienced as an emotion. Do you think that this extensive, differentiated experience can really be passed on?*

That is quite a difficult question.

Question: *Before you answer, let me give you the word 'solidarity' as a kind of clue. You were in no doubt struck by the fact that during the coup in Chile, it took young people a few days to absorb what was happening and to lend their solidarity.*

I think that your book addresses a problem: isn't solidarity – looking at it as thoroughly as we possibly can from our own point of view, particularly in connection with Chile – merely rationality? Can we appreciate it emotionally at all, for reasons of geographical remoteness, national development and cultural atmosphere? And this poses the question, is the problem of fascism comprehensible to us today in the way you raise it? To this extent I think your book has a lot to say to us, but I think that the problem can be approached on other levels than the purely rational, and I think your dream is symptomatic of this, I mean the dream with the swing. It is a dream you could have, but I couldn't. And since I couldn't have this dream, I couldn't have any deep-seated emotional attitude to Chile, only a rational attitude.

Your book will probably bring back many memories and rouse many feelings in its readers. Nevertheless I ask, can our young people understand fascism in an emotional way? I mean, rationally, it is obvious what its origins were, economically, politically, socially – that's no big deal, we've been through all that. And it's something that should be said again and again; I'm not against that. But, emotionally, I don't think it's accessible to us.

Further question: *I would like to add something to that. The problem of the absence of emotion in solidarity that has been raised here doesn't, in my opinion, have its origins in different cultural environments but largely in the strict way this movement towards solidarity has been channelled.*

Yes, I agree with you. You are right to sense from the excerpt – and the whole book is like this – that I try to break through the purely rational communication of knowledge or experience. This is not because I am anti-rational in any way – I certainly am not – but because I have been through this particular experience. I have, of course, been thinking a lot recently about when and how you not merely came to understand, but when something new really did begin to stir inside you, a new quality in your potential for life and action. This always happened in situations when an emotion had been set in motion. It seems to me that where the past is concerned, in particular this part of our past – but the same applies to other periods of time we have experienced – we have filtered our emotions out too much. They are left standing alongside knowledge, but outside it; one is alone with them. This has to do with the fact that the intellectual realization that one has made a mistake is easier to bear than the emotion of shame, and it is less difficult to acquire precise knowledge than to feel things 'correctly'. The one without the other, though, produces remarkably split personalities, as we can see around us.

I mentioned our history textbooks and how they handle fascism. One day, our younger daughter asked us, 'Who was this man Eichmann, then?' We were horrified that it was possible for her not to know that. Her history book really didn't mention his name at all. So there has been no attempt, probably not in German language and literature textbooks either, to make young people aware of this character type, the *Schreibtischmörder* – the 'desk-murderers' – or to explain what kind of historical development can pave the way for the rise to power of this type of person, or how such a thing could come about at all on German soil. Kazimierz Brandys, a Pole, said: 'fascism exists all over the world, but the Germans were its classic exponents'.

This was one of the comments which finally spurred me into writing this book. I realized straight away that he was right. It's true, you could imagine almost any country having its own brand of dictator, its own Hitler. Himmler and Eichmann, on the other hand, are very special inventions, able to assume power in a specific country in specific circumstances. One really must reflect further on this and try to get to the bottom of it.

There is a question I cannot answer definitively: to what extent can one generation pass on its experiences to the next? But, first, we must ask to what extent it actually tries to? More could be done on this than is being done at the moment, either than we are doing or than the previous generation did with us.

Personally, I was lucky. When I was still quite young, although already an adult, I met people who were not in any way Nazis and who told me more about this time than has appeared, or could have appeared, in the newspapers or history books – or indeed than was to be found in their own books, for some of them were writers. This was very important for me. But I came to realize for the first time when I began writing that this meant I was left with a kind of 'no man's land' between the two eras in my life, that is between my childhood, let's say up to sixteen years of age, and a new stage when I developed what could be crudely termed a 'new world view'. These two eras, which in themselves are quite clear and distinct, are separated by a colourless intervening period. These are all problems connected with emotionality, thus with what one really experiences and learns from emotions. In our country generally, and I mean in the family as well, we do not allow strong feelings to intrude into a child's upbringing. We try to avoid too much feeling at all costs. Whatever you do, don't get excited, don't burst into tears when someone is murdered on the TV and don't, whatever you do, let this interrupt supper!

I think that a lot that happens in the world is allowed to occur because we lack vision, because our powers of imagination are too weak to allow us to put ourselves in the position of the people to whom it is happening. But the smaller the world becomes through technology, the more important it becomes to develop the virtue of empathy with what is alien to us. And really this virtue can be practised in any moderately good book, because literature, among other things, ought to do precisely this: exercise our imagination, develop our vision. In this case, this means learning to relate the history of one's own people, one's own class, to one's own life, so that contemporary history finds us capable of proper feelings and able to act according to our own judgement.

Question: *Do you view the world from a literary standpoint or are there several people inside you who all react differently to the present?*

The briefest reply, and the one I would most like to give, would be 'No – I do not have a literary approach to the present.' It would also be broadly true, because those events, processes or actions which I am drawn into, by which I am moved particularly profoundly, I experience in an absolutely 'unliterary' way. What I mean is that I don't have any sense of being an observer. I never think. 'Aha!, you should write about that,' or, 'He would make a good character'. That doesn't come into it at all. Anything experienced in such a calculating way is, in my opinion, spoilt and unuseable 'material'.

I must confess, though, that being a writer does leave its mark. There are moments and periods of heightened calm in which you reflect on your experiences. You have a sense of viewing things differently, even when they are happening, from how you would have had you not been a writer. This is a remarkable thing. It is simply a fact that if you write, even if it is only one book every ten years, yet see yourself the whole time as a writer, then you live differently from how you would if you just lived normally, and then at some point or other wrote a book, but then never wrote another and writing played no further role in your life.

Your powers of observation are heightened, you feel a continual pressure of responsibility, a constant commitment. All these feelings are incredibly strong and come down to the fact that, whether you like it or not, you are there to describe your experiences. From a certain point onwards, it is pointless being rational enough to take a realistic view of your own contribution to literature, not to overestimate it. It is immaterial whether you are very good or not really all that good. The simple fact that you know you are there to describe your experience, makes a great difference.

Question: *Your books always make a great impression on me. Sometimes I wonder what effect your work has on other people. What do you feel is the effect of your books? Are you able to assess what you will achieve with them from the outset?*

The effect varies. There are readers who react in the same way as you, but there are others who think I ought to be put away – someone said exactly that to me once, word for word. Those are two extreme reactions. Between these extremes, there is a lot of friendly agreement and interest, even sometimes a kind of long-term involvement where readers will return to a book which they either didn't really like first time round or found too difficult. But I think this is probably the same with almost every author.

Many of the letters I receive show that some readers, especially women, identify with particular characters, and sometimes feel a stronger bond than I would or could feel. These reactions cannot be anticipated in advance. I don't know why a particular book or figure at a particular moment encounters a great number of people who feel particularly affected by it. It has to do with a particular social atmosphere and the particular stage of development people find themselves at, which coincides with that of the author when she was writing the book. This is something one realizes in retrospect.

A lot of readers write to me. Or I learn what effect my books have on people of different age-groups and different sexes from conversations like this one here today. But to be honest I try to forget this again and remain as independent as I possibly can, because it would be fatal to imagine the effect on different groups of readers while you are writing. It doesn't work. You must really free yourself of this, 'as if' (in inverted commas) you had never written anything before, 'as if' you had never listened to readers' judgements, either negative or positive. You must try every day to re-establish this freedom, to avoid feeling pressurised by an existing readership – though on the other hand, you would be unhappy to lose it.

Question (asked by Wieland Herzfelde)*: *Most writers returning from emigration had little idea about who was really to blame. How should those who had let themselves get more seriously embroiled in it be treated, and what about the whole issue of the young people, the children, the teenagers? And I think we failed to comprehend that because the world stage had been completely reconstructed (it seemed to be such a total change at that time, though it has now turned out to be not so total after all), these people no longer knew how they ought to react. In the days when I was still lecturing, someone once came up to me and said, 'Listen, what you say about the fight against the Nazis and everything else, I understand what you're saying, but you know there's more to it than that, you can't just rub yourself out and start again . . .' And this is where the problem we were talking about comes up . . . . 'Look,' she said, 'for me it's like this. As a child in Nazi Germany I also had a lot of fun. And whatever you think of, whether it be an excursion, a sports festival or a family event, it all happened against a background and, surprising though it may seem, the most enjoyable experiences were always associated with the swastika flag. Now of course I know, as everyone does today, what that flag stood for, but it doesn't help me. I still remember my friend and I getting home late and getting into trouble . . . . Yes, we went off walking, I had a really good time then, walking and sport were great fun, but there was always a swastika flag there.' And the woman didn't really know what she ought to do to make her memories of this terrible time seem terrible, because she had a lot of nice memories, or at least memories which didn't fit into the scheme of those who were anti-fascist from the beginning.*

---

*Wieland Herzfelde (b.1896, Switzerland) studied at Berlin University; member of KPD; head of Malik publishing house, Berlin; joined SED; became Professor of Sociology at Karl-Marx University, Leipzig, and member of the German Academy of Arts – Tr.

And here I think we, the older generation, made a definite mistake in thinking that if young people were given the best books written by the best anti-fascists, then we would be giving them weapons with which they could fight their own memories. It doesn't work. And because of this, I think the book (although I don't know it in any detail yet or what happens at the end) does a very necessary job of creating a better understanding between the older and younger generation, who, though they bore no guilt for Hitler's fascism, somehow had to share the guilt which was churned up in his war and the numerous atrocities, because naturally everybody they associated with were, to a greater or lesser extent, Nazis. I think that the book is a very honest one, and I suspect it will prove to be a useful one.

Question: *That would be a good place to end, but I would like to add a further question. Actually I would like to quote something from an article by Fritz Cremer* which no doubt many of you are familiar with. He says: 'I think that as a Communist one is duty bound to openly discuss the most difficult problems.' In the GDR some artists make concessions to the official line. Others try to go their own way and end up in confrontation with official opinion. I think that these are matters of the gravest concern. I want to ask, then, if you have come across these difficulties? Have you yourself ever got into difficulty with the official line? Are you expecting criticism of your new book? How would you respond to such criticism?*

That's a lot of questions at one go. It would take us all night to discuss that.

Response: *We've got all night!*

All right, then. You know, if you had asked me that say four or five years ago, then I would have reacted with great vigour and emotion. Now I have come to react less emotionally and I don't think this is because I have been drawn into what you called 'the official line' or what Fritz Cremer perhaps meant – four years ago, was it, when he gave his interview?[†] The date is important. It is important whether it was said today or four years ago, because Fritz Cremer would no longer use this term or see any absolute antithesis between the 'official line' and what one is trying to express in art. The reason for this is that for the last four years, as you may or may not know, there has been greater room for manoeuvre (perhaps not the

---

*Fritz Cremer (b. 1902, Westphalia), sculptor; moved to Berlin late 1920s; member of KPD and co-founder of Red Students' Union; member of SED – Tr.

[†]The interview in question was first published in the Danish newspaper *Land og Folk.* Extracts were reprinted in *Der Spiegel,* 3 May 1971.

best expression for the context) – there have been more opportunities to take up problems, to express conflicts which we could not broach before, at least not in this way. Nobody stops you writing. To this extent one cannot see the relationship between art and politics ahistorically or statically. One must examine it in a concrete historical way.

But that doesn't really solve the fundamental question. The basic question is not whether an 'official line' forbids this or that. That has happened in the past and will happen again and, to my mind, it is a very superficial and rather tedious way of looking at things. Today you might have read, in connection with the production of Goethe's *Tasso*, that Goethe wrote the play in the 1780s but wasn't allowed to perform it until 1807 at the Weimar court. Now, he hardly went round incensed with rage, complaining that he couldn't perform his play. That's no attitude to take. It's much more difficult to acquire and develop a productive attitude. It's easy to say, I won't write anything else, that'll teach them. It's much more difficult not to do that, to remain productive and fair-minded. As to whether I am expecting criticism, of course I am. In fact I am expecting all kinds of different criticism and hopefully some of it will be productive, highlighting the points that really can be criticised. But even if it doesn't, there will be criticism and all kinds of things will be said, some of which I could tell you now, since they are always coming up. But all this is relatively unimportant. What is important is that individual people themselves, either in groups, like here tonight for example, or in smaller circles of friends, or with individual readers, can acquire and preserve a creative attitude. This means that you don't get discouraged, or at least not persistently discouraged, by what is mostly temporary stupidity, which can at times be very powerful, even vicious. You don't need to tell me about this, I am quite aware of it.

On the other hand, life is really rather short, and if you spend four or five years of your life getting annoyed about things that get in your way, then those five years are gone for good and at some point you have to realize that. At some point you have to grasp that you're there to say quite specific things – the value of which I don't overestimate in my own case, by the way. You have to say these things regardless of what this or that politician or this or that newspaper thinks or writes, regardless too of what the majority of readers think about it. And by no means the worst or least well known of our colleagues, in the past, have had to wait years or decades with things that were very important to them, but which they wrote in a time that had no use for them.

So I think that once we are no longer little children, it is really up to us to show a cetain poise, and stride out into the space provided for us in this country, which I see above all as a field of productive tensions between author and reader. And we cannot complain that we have not been given the opportunity to enter into a productive relationship with those who are interested in what we are doing. Of course, this doesn't only mean those who agree with you, but those who are keen to learn, who want to rub up against your work and add their own thoughts on it or say, 'No, that's not what I think about this'. They're quite entitled to do so. And then you get the feeling that there's another force in play, that we aren't just two smooth surfaces slipping past each other but that some kind of cogwheel is engaged, that something is moving with us, indirectly – which is the only way literature ever can be effective.

In my opinion one should treat this public sphere with great respect. I'm not talking about any 'official line' now, but about the public sphere. And in the GDR, the public sphere is quite well developed. Even if it is not articulated in newspapers as one would like it to be, it exists in a lot of other places, including readers' letters. I have never felt isolated even in those periods when my name was not being mentioned in the papers. For this reason, I have never felt the need to deceive these readers either. That is one half of the story. The other half, and I don't want to play this down in any way, is that a period when opinions which are grossly stupid, hostile and alien to art prevail and are advocated everywhere naturally has an inhibiting effect on production, even if you try to arm yourself against it. You simply waste too much energy opposing this instead of using that energy productively and progressively. It is also easy then to become un-critical of yourself, because if you are forced constantly to defend yourself against stupid criticisms, then those which are right and justified, which you ought to assimilate, no longer get through. You stop criticizing your colleagues because, if they are constantly being criticized on grounds you don't agree with, you stop putting your own criticisms forward as you perhaps ought to. And the same applies to the way they treat me.

What I'm trying to say is that a time like the one we have experienced has inhibited and discouraged art. But there's no point crying about this or imagining that the struggle for realism in art will ever get easy or come to an end.

Question: *When is your book due to be published?*

It all depends on me really, on when I deliver it. But it is scheduled for the end of 1976. Printing takes a long time. If it gets to the publishers in January or February, for instance, it won't appear until November, I think.

Question: *You said that you also wanted to contribute something to the process of coming to term with our past, our history. Why then are the contemporary illustrations you use from countries like Chile, America and Vietnam and not from socialist countries?*

As I said earlier, other chapters take different examples. It's not so one-sided. The biggest shock in terms of fascist and fascistic developments, to which I was particularly receptive and which particularly concerned me when I was writing the book, happened to come from these countries. This I took up in the book. And something else which concerned me, and still does, is my trip to America and what I witnessed there. These are things which relate to what I was doing personally at the time. But I understand what you mean and you are absolutely right, that what concerns us in our countries, what produces inner tension here and what we argue amongst ourselves about, must naturally be given form. The question is simply when, how and where? Personally, I think I can say that I don't intend to avoid the issue.

Question: *Does your novel also contain analyses of our politics, possibly in some of the other passages which we didn't get to hear today?*

Yes. As I said, it does, but it would be pointless for me to extract them now and tell you about them. There are a few passages, because obviously memory can't be channelled into a single track. I am deliberately laying the main emphasis in this period, but I think in later books the subsequent phase must be treated. I don't necessarily mean in books like this one, but I am very aware that much of the post-1945 period is equally 'unmastered' and still to be written about. But you have to create foundations that you define personally on which you can build.

1975

4

THE SAND AND PINES OF BRANDENBURG

A Conversation with Adam Krzemiński*

Adam Krzemiński: *For centuries German literature was a male literature, created by and for men. When female characters did appear, in Lessing, Goethe, Schlegel or Theodor Fontane, they were simply reflections of the conflicts within patriarchal society.*

Yes, you're right, though we should not forget our own Annette von Droste-Hülshoff writing in the first half of the last century, or the role Rahel Varnhagen's salons played in the post-Napoleonic period.

Adam Krzemiński: *Anyhow, I would say that this male reign reached its zenith in the aphorisms and misogyny of Nietzsche. In the twentieth century, especially since the Second World War, many of the key literary works in the German language have been written by women. In Austria by Ingeborg Bachmann, in West Germany by Angelika Mechtel, Gabriele Wohmann and most recently Karin Struck, in the GDR by Brigitte Reimann, Sarah Kirsch, Irmtraud Morgner and, above all, by yourself.*

Above all by Anna Seghers!

Adam Krzemiński: *We'll come back to Anna Seghers. First of all, I would like to ask whether all these women can be seen as together having brought some new quality to literature?*

I am surprised by your thesis that German literature has been essentially 'male', though I am certainly willing to accept it. I agree too on the point

---

*Originally published in *Polityka*, no. 2, 1976. Present version from the German translation by Stanislawa Diersch.

that these women, though working in very different circumstances, are all united by one thing – their conscious effort to introduce emotionality into literature, and their clash with what is still a patriarchal society.

Adam Krzemiński: *Despite emancipation?*

That word has been used too often to have much meaning any more and, characteristically, Ingeborg Bachmann warns us against the dangers of pseudo-emancipation. In one of her last interviews she said that all men were sick, but they just didn't know it yet.

Adam Krzemiński: *Is that your opinion too?*

Not really. I would put it somewhat differently. Men have been particularly distorted by the social conditions that have prevailed up to the present. Both in the past and today they have been under pressure to achieve, to have a successful career. This makes it particularly difficult for them to break free of the frustrating compulsion to accumulate both possessions and status. Women, on the other hand, who were denied any social role and so remained outside these mechanisms, have retained a greater sensitivity and – something we should not feel ashamed of – a greater spontaneity and a separate, more human scale of values.

Adam Krzemiński: *Values which are being strengthened by an increasing self-awareness?*

By the conviction that these moral values can save our lives. I say 'our' because I also include men in this.

Adam Krzemiński: *And how do these moral values relate to social and political values?*

You can see extremely well how the two come together in discussions with readers, including discussions with young men. They realize that they are being offered new forms of co-existence demanding completely new qualities, not the ability to push your way to the top, to outdo your partner. We're talking about a way of living together which doesn't exclude tenderness, sensitivity, brotherliness – or if you prefer 'sister-liness'. These moral values are extraordinarily relevant to society today.

Adam Krzemiński: *These are values which relate to one's inner life, one's inner feelings?*

Not exclusively.

Adam Krzemiński: *To one's self-confidence too?*

Above all to one's self-realization (*Selbstverwirklichung*). Just take a look at the poetry written by women. It is filled with a sadness produced by lack of fulfilment, but also with a sense of great expectation. It seems to me that men abandon their expectations much more quickly; they conform sooner; they 'understand' what is permissible and what is not. Women, perhaps for historical or perhaps for other reasons, do not give up their dreams so easily.... Maybe they have not yet been exposed long enough to the treadmill of production and hierarchy for their senses to have been as dulled as many men's.

Adam Krzemiński: *This is also important in relation to the conflicts portrayed in literature in the GDR. A common theme of many novels is a woman's abandonment of her husband as she becomes disappointed by his conformism and opportunism....*

In real life too it is young women who find marriage particularly difficult. The high divorce rate must tell us something.

Adam Krzemiński: *Is it that men have lost their identity and become weaker and less convincing in their role? For historical, cultural and psychological reasons?*

Men have lost their self-confidence and the conviction that their world and their social role are inviolable. Today we see certain traditional values – be strong, conform, make a career – being challenged. These values are still highly regarded by society, but not quite so highly by women. I think that this further increases the stress men are under. Their position is not an enviable one. For this reason I never sit in judgement on men. Quite the reverse. I believe that, in time, women must come to realize that they should help men rather than run away from them. Help them, not by aiding their careers, but by discovering a new partnership based on human friendship.

Adam Krzemiński: *This is a very interesting state of affairs, one that is somewhat at variance with our experience in Poland. Our literature has been more influenced by women than is the case in Germany. It could also be that women have occupied a much higher position in our society. This is connected partly with the Catholic cult of the Virgin Mary, and partly with the social and political situation in nineteenth-century Poland. Firstly, men were unable to protect their land and their wives from those who conquered the country, so the male role was called into question. Secondly, women were the mainstays not only of those families ruined by uprisings and deportations, but also of culture. At the end of the nineteenth century Polish literature lay securely in the hands of women: Orzeszkowa, Nalkowka, Dabrowska. Few men could match their perceptiveness or strength of character. . . .*

In our case, the male role was not undermined until after the Second World War. For this reason, an aversion to men and a determination to assert themselves prevailed for a time amongst a number of German-speaking women writers, like Irmtraud Morgner for example.

Adam Krzemiński: *To prove that they were better men?*

Yes. First of all to show that we could be tractor drivers, sailors, etc. Only now have we learned that the social and economic foundations of emancipation, though extremely important, are not everything. Only now have we realized that we should not have followed in men's footsteps, as this has led to the destruction of 'feminine' qualities.

Adam Krzemiński: *Like motherhood, for example. I find it surprising how the problem of bringing up one's own children is treated as a secondary issue in East German literature and cinema. The TV serial* The Seven Affairs of Donna Juanita *was shown on Polish television. It followed the seven amorous adventures of a single woman, whose own child was more of a burden than a source of any more profound experience.*

I saw that too. Although the film contained some good observations, it ignored the main problems facing women – perhaps because it was conceived by men. Innumerable conversations with women have strengthened my conviction that many working women feel a sense of guilt towards their children. This problem has not been solved at all.

Adam Krzemiński: *But back to literature. Earlier I deliberately left out Anna Seghers because for me she is the 'last man' amongst women writers. Her novels have a thoroughly 'male' feel to them; they are laden with categorical statements and definitive truths. This is obvious even in their titles – 'Die Entscheidung' ('The Decision'), 'Das Vertrauen' ('Trust'). The tone of these novels is very different from your own, which are full of reflection, contemplation, speculation. . . .*

That's true.

Adam Krzemiński: *Perhaps today the differences between Anna Seghers and Willi Bredel or Hans Marchwitza are fading.*

But these differences are still very clear. They are all of the same generation though. Anna Seghers comes from a bourgeois family and came out in support of both the workers' movement and the Communist Party very early on. I think that decision left its mark. Except for a few autobiographical works, she keeps herself completely out of her literature. Her objectivity almost reaches the point of self-suppression. Her asceticism is deliberate. She wrote what she thought had to be written at the time.

Adam Krzemiński: *Nevertheless, Anna Seghers is very close to you. Is this the mutual attraction of opposite poles?*

Not mutual. I'm very attached to some of her books like *Transit* or *Der Ausflug der toten Mädchen.* When I got to know her I was a young journalist in awe of a great writer. Later, our contacts with each other grew stronger. Anna Seghers was very interested in the experiences of my generation. We simply talked to each other about ourselves. I owe her a great deal.

Adam Krzemiński: *And what is Anna Seghers's opinion of your approach to literature?*

She is loyal but not uncritical. She did like *The Quest for Christa T.* and always defended it, possibly because it depicts the life of a different generation. I think she is sceptical about my approach, though. She doesn't like things being stripped down to their essence, she prefers a kind of classical restraint. She would never have done anything of this kind herself – I am thinking here of the merciless questioning of things which, in her view, would not be up for discussion. Incidentally, this is a position that I both understand and respect. Seen from the point of view of Anna Seghers's development, it is understandable and necessary.

Adam Krzemiński: *And what do you make of Anna Seghers's position in the thirties, the theoretical battles which, like Brecht and Bloch, she conducted with Lukács?*

When I studied German at the beginning of the fifties, for us Lukács was sacrosanct. Thus, in interpreting the argument between Anna Seghers and Lukács, we had respect for her but deferred to him, since it was Lukács who saw the future of the socialist novel as being to reproduce the achievements of the great bourgeois novel and German classicism, to reflect reality in its totality. My sympathy for Anna Seghers only developed later as a result of her undogmatic defence of those writers, like Lenz or Kleist, for whom reality with all its contradictions did not come together in an Olympian image.

Adam Krzemiński: *In the thirties she had already rehabilitated the 'failures' of German literature, with all their madness, sickness and fever. And yet, this influenced her own work in only a very minor way.*

The influence wasn't all that minor. Just think of *Aufstand der Fischer von St Barbara* or her short stories. But basically you're right. She did not want to expose herself to the same danger, but she did understand what it meant for writers to be steeped in the conflicts of their age – take Hölderlin and Dostoevsky. To this day, she treats Goethe with great respect, but also with detachment. Lukács and many of his disciples simply could not understand this. It is only now that our attitude to Goethe is becoming more sophisticated. . . .

Adam Krzemiński: *Once, at a conference in West Berlin, you were accused by dogmatists of the radical left of giving in to bourgeois individualism. The answer you gave then interests me because our young critics too sometimes accuse young poets of a similar thing.*

Well yes ... literature in West Germany too has gone through various stages. At the time when I was in West Berlin, the young intellectuals who regarded themselves as being on the far left had just begun to discuss social issues in literature. This was indeed important and necessary. But we had already been through this phase in the fifties; for us, social commitment is something that is taken for granted. The issue for us now is the literary form this committment takes, how it can be deepened and broadened. I answered the accusations at the time by saying that we should at that particular moment discuss the problems of man's inner development and the human psyche. In my opinion this is the most important task for literature and is, indeed, a political task – one which does not necessarily lead to 'spiritualization'. The young people at the conference were not prepared to see this, because they did not get beyond our own critical analysis of the fifties. It was as if we had come full circle. Only with enormous effort had we shaken off our dogmatism and arrived at questions which no longer ignored the individual. Then suddenly, from an unexpected quarter, we were faced with equally dogmatic and simplistic reproaches, fuelled by the kind of arguments we ourselves had used years before. Much to my regret, I could not identify with these young people. I remembered the discussions we used to have on how a literature centred on the individual was harmful, on how showing sorrow disarmed us and led to passivity. It has become clear now that this was wrong, that society cannot be understood unless we rediscover the way to ourselves, unless authors reflect and contemplate.

Adam Krzemiński: *The environment plays an important role in your novels. You are bound to a particular landscape. In your writing one can feel the sand and pines of Brandenburg....*

... You are thinking of *The Quest for Christa T.* which was based on a specific incident. Incidentally this is also typical of the landscape of Mecklenburg.

Adam Krzemiński: *But also 'Unter den Linden'.*

Certainly my books are set against the particular background of Brandenburg and Berlin. Sand and pine forests are part of my childhood memories. I was born in Landsberg an der Warthe, which is now Gorzow. After that I lived in Saxony, Thüringia and Mecklenburg, but I still feel most at home amongst sand and pine forest.

Adam Krzemiński: *And in a particular literary tradition. It is surely no coincidence that you take up the work of Fontane, Storm and E.T.A. Hoffmann. You have even written a new version of* Lebensansichten des Katers Murr. *These authors define a certain spiritual territory, but certainly not a political one....*

... meaning ...

Adam Krzemiński: *Prussia. I mean Prussia as a particular intellectual tradition, not as goose-stepping and uniforms. Is something of old Prussia, however intangible, still alive? Has any of its tradition, mentality or atmosphere survived?*

Of course some of it has survived, otherwise there would be no difference between us and the Poles. Efficiency, obedience and sobriety are usually taken to be the typical Prussian characteristics. But there's more to it than that. Today in old Prussian Berlin, you can easily detect romantic desires. This is because Romanticism, although repressed, was still a popular current even in Prussia and was able to keep alive 'un-Prussian' qualities like a sense of beauty and – though this may sound ridiculous – charm.

Adam Krzemiński: *What forms does this romantic yearning take?*

It comes out in a certain attitude, perhaps noticeable in Warsaw too.... At any rate, it is there in that sobriety which in Berlin you find mixed with a longing to make life richer: that sense of abundance and yet of insatiability. This is apparent above all in the passionate interest in culture, art, literature and the probing questioning of the value of one's own life. Let me give you a concrete example. In a small town which recently sprang up in the middle of the Brandenburg sand – a lot of new housing blocks with a department store in the middle – a spontaneously formed group of people who were intellectually active, came completely to dominate cultural life there. They began, at first privately, to invite writers and other interesting people to the town. Operating outside the usual channels for the dissemination of culture, they organized lectures and exhibitions by artists who were often not yet recognized and who had not yet appeared on television. Today this group officially runs the cultural life of the town. It has acquired contracts with two theatres and sponsorship of a school. They have not, in the process, had to abandon their style. They offered their social environment a fresh, new and direct approach to community life. Many different kinds of people are involved: workers, teachers, technicians, doctors. Like Baron von Münchhausen they have pulled themselves up, by their own bootstraps, out of the drudgery of the daily round.

Another problem is that we are gradually discovering a new sense of national identity – and one that is not always of the best sort, I might add. In all this, we have to make up for past failings, come to terms with what has been suppressed and get over the severe crisis our attitude to our national tradition has been through.

Adam Krzemiński: *That is already under way. Talking to young East Germans today, you can sense an interest of this kind in their origins, their natural environment, their past. The interest in oneself, which we were just speaking of, stimulates interest also in one's surroundings. Here in Poland, we also seek our identity through our history....*

This isn't easy, on account of the dual relationship of Prussia and Germany to history. On the one hand, there is the rejection of the militaristic Prussian state, which we don't want to have anything to do with, and on the other the many intertwining threads of historical development which one cannot deny. In a town like Potsdam, these stand out as clearly as the lines on the palm of your hand. In fact until recently the town had never been fully rebuilt and there were even plans to demolish some historic buidings. Now they are being restored by Polish specialists, who have shown how it should be done in cities like Gdansk. A visit to Sanssouci, the summer residence of Frederick II, will show you how our relationship to history has been shaken. The guide barely whispers his name, yet he is willing to talk at great length about Voltaire. The relationship with the past is, however, more harmonious, in old Saxony – for example in Dresden or Leipzig.

Adam Krzemiński: *This interest in history comes out in your own work too. I am thinking of the film script you wrote with your husband.*

And which has now been filmed. We really wanted to portray a young person who is thrown into life completely unprepared, who is suddenly placed at the centre of a great historical process.

Adam Krzemiński: *In the thick of things. . . .*

A person incapable of rising to the challenge of the times, who does not possess the intellectual or material means to do so, but who, with time, nevertheless develops common sense and loses his illusions. He does not become a drop-out, though, or a cynic. He does not collapse under the strain, but gradually acquires understanding, In a world of cold dogmatists and inflamed religious fanatics he begins to find space to move freely. He knows everything, he understands everything.

Adam Krzemiński: *But he must keep his healthy understanding to himself. 'Till Eulenspiegel' is a journey in time, a journey into the past. But in your two futurological short stories 'Selbstversuch' and 'Neue Lebensansichten eines Katers' you travel into the future. How are these time-travels related to the present?*

In our version, Till Eulenspiegel? is a prototype intellectual, who in his own day could only play the role of court jester because of the restrictions placed on him by the various competing parties. Though this is not a direct allusion to the present, there are connections. In the two futurological stories, on the other hand, I was interested in the responsibility which science has towards people. Transposing the philistine, in the figure of the cat Murr, into the future allowed me to throw some current problems into relief. These journeys in time make it possible to understand the present better. For I am convinced that my main work will be devoted to the present, to the question of how the individual stands the test of extreme historical circumstances.

Adam Krzemiński: *You are approaching this in your latest book,* A Model Childhood, *which as yet we know only from fragments.*

This is a reflection on the present through the medium of history. Of course we already have a wealth of literature on German fascism, including works by authors of my generation. However, I wanted to consider and describe what goes on inside a child at such times, what makes an indelible mark on its memory and what it suppresses and why. The book is devoted to the past, but it is set in present day Gorzow and I describe a journey to that town. Ten years ago I could not have written it.

Adam Krzemiński: *Just as Christa T. was unable to complete her story, her recollection of her journey in 1940 to conquered Poland, to the town where her father worked for the occupying authorities. Are you in a way continuing Christa T.'s story?*

It is rather that I am taking up the threads she left. I have often said in my writing that we have to rethink the experiences our generation went through. I have worked on this for many years and I have constantly found new things to say about it. I often quote Kazimierz Brandys in *A Model Childhood*, by the way, because some of what he says is exactly how I would say it, or at least would hope to. For example, Brandys writes that fascism was a worldwide phenomenon, that the Germans were merely its classic exponents. And the real sense of my book is my reflection on this. A Hitler could perhaps emerge in other countries as well, whereas Eichmann and Himmler are typical German expressions of the fascist bureaucrat. And in seeking out the source of this irrational perversity, I am also questioning what we feel about it today. In this sense I think I have written a book about the present.

1976

5

LITERARY WORK IN THE GDR

An Interview With Richard A. Zipser*

Richard Zipser: *What do you consider to be the role of art and literature in a socialist state?*

So long as we have a division of labour, it will be the specialist role of writers to create a self-awareness for their age and society, to give it a sense of its own identity. This will be the case whether they – or others – see themselves this way or not. German literary history is full of examples of how the offerings of the most important writers were rejected by their contemporaries. The common fate of J.M.R. Lenz, Friedrich Hölderlin, Heinrich von Kleist and Georg Büchner, their decline into poverty, madness and suicide, are illustrations of what Marx called 'the German plight', of a historical evolution which, having prevented the development of any revolutionary movement after the suppression of the Peasant Wars of the sixteenth century, eventually resulted in the emergence of a bourgeoisie too weak to create a national state. This historical process gave rise to particularly acute forms of alienation between writers and their potential readers.

Socialist literature in Germany can, I think, help overcome this alienation though it cannot, in the process, step outside of German history or escape from its consequences. In 1945, when German fascism was conquered, not by the opposition of the German people but by the allied troops, a radically new phase of history began on what today is the territory of the GDR. But there was no 'zero hour'. Like anyone else, we writers in the GDR find ourselves within a political force-field conditioned

---

*Responses to a written questionnaire prepared by the German Department of Oberlin College, Oberlin, Ohio. Originally published in R.A. Zipser, *DDR im Tauwetter*, vol. III (New York, Bern, Frankfurt am Main 1985).

by social and historical factors. We too are bound by the conditions set by history, time and place. Here, literature has the same function as it has had for more than two thousand years in 'the West': it expresses the tensions between the demands, needs, hopes and desires of individuals and those of their society. Completely contented people do not need art. It is true that socialist authors proceed from certain objectives, which have, incidentally, tended at times to be taken for realities. In socialist countries, property relations have been fundamentally transformed and, for this reason, so too have human relations and moral precepts. Yet we too live in a hierarchically ordered, economically-orientated society which retains the old, harsh mode of production. I consider it our role to measure the reality of our society against its professed goals and to keep alive the longing for that realistic utopia in which we could live together in a truly 'human', i.e. productive way.

Richard Zipser: *With which contemporary social problems are you most concerned as a writer?*

The relations between the new social strata which have emerged from our conditions here interest me greatly. I am keen to get at the causes of certain distortions which I have observed in the conduct of intellectuals and leading economic and political figures of my generation: for example, their attitude towards their wives – or husbands – and children, fellow-workers, pupils, trainees, friends and colleagues. I am curious to know what conditions produce obsequiousness, conformism, mistrust, the compulsion to succeed and the inability to feel love and grief. I don't observe these phenomena in a remote, detached manner, as a sociologist might; I have to call my own self into question as I write. My approach is subjective, but at the same time social; for that reason, I can't strictly say which 'social phenomena' I deal with.

Richard Zipser: *Does your work treat the theme of women in society?*

I don't consider 'women in society' simply as one theme amongst many. I write almost exclusively about women, but I wouldn't call my writing 'emancipation literature'; that would be too restrictive a label. My interest lies not so much in equality for women – legal and economic equality is guaranteed by our legislation – as in their self-realization in a specific historical situation, since their self-consciousness, what they demand of life, goes beyond the opportunities society offers them. Women, who have been less disfigured than many men by the pressure to compete and achieve which industrial society has exerted for generations, are increasingly striving for new, more convivial ways of living, for a full and complete life (and not just for higher production figures). From this emerges a wealth of potential conflict which is principally dealt with in literature, because other media treat it too rarely and too superficially, rushing to announce that real changes have taken place when as yet only the foundations for change have been laid and old practices and customs remain untouched. I am fascinated by those women who recognize and seize the historical moment presented to them, no matter how difficult that might be. They are able earlier than most men to articulate how a new way of life and a new era might feel. They are not interested in what they have, but in who they are. They can do what men do, but they are beginning to ask themselves if that is really what they want. They are questioning the constraints of an achievement-orientated society and, with the maturity gained from discussing real, meaningful experiences, they have given voice to a radically new demand: that they be allowed to make use of all their senses and abilities. And the hard-headed vision they have gained from taking their share in responsibility is not so easily clouded by deluded political thinking as is that of so many men, whose view of things in this man's world is less grounded in reality. They have not – not yet at least – become so easily enslaved by that 'Reason' which is so self-deceiving and pretends that the problems facing twentieth-century humanity are simply technical and that suddenly the global confusion of ends and means, that mysticism which pretends to want good and yet creates evil, could after all turn a world bristling with arms into one desiring peace. I have found that women have a more rational approach to these 'big' issues than the men who in fact decide them. It is for this reason, because they are capable of a greater degree of humanity, that I write about women.

Richard Zipser: *What influence have the experiences of your own youth had on your work?*

When I was sixteen, fascism was defeated in Germany. That was one of the most devastating experiences of my life and led me constantly to try and analyze my childhood. It was only later, however, in the seventies, that this became the central subject of one of my books, *A Model Childhood*, which appeared in German in 1976. The way my character was shaped during my childhood and early youth, and, above all, the critical analysis of fascism, to which I was uncritically delivered up as a child, decisively determined my later political commitment and sensitized me to all shades of terror, violence, irrationalism, mass hysteria and demagogy. The mechanisms by which large masses of people are seduced into committing acts of extreme barbarism against minorities concern me greatly, as does the role of technology in creating new forms of barbarism.

Richard Zipser: *How have you gained experience with workers? What links do you have with them today?*

For many years, I had direct links with an enterprise, with brigades and with workers' writing groups. Now, I spend half the year in the country-side, where, living alongside workers and co-operative farmers, I am able to develop closer contact with them in a way that I couldn't in a city. I don't regard these relations as 'material' for my writing, though. The characters in one of my earlier books are workers, but now I think that particular environments, particular ways of thinking and feeling, can only be described in all their complexity by people who are at home in those environments, who are, for example, workers themselves. Of course, you need to know about their lives and their problems for *any* form of literary work, whether it directly concerns workers or not. I would hope that every book that addresses contemporary issues is of interest to them.

Richard Zipser: *What peculiar qualities do you think GDR literature has within the German-speaking world?*

GDR literature, provided it is true to life, can communicate experiences which are not available to authors in the Federal Republic, Austria or Switzerland: experiences of a society which does not produce on the basis of the private ownership of the means of production, individual profit and competition. The fact that authors identify with the basic principles of this society does not temper, but in fact brings out more sharply, the conflicts that have been caused by certain distortions in the GDR, and these have indeed provoked fundamental debate within our literature. There is an impetus within GDR literature actively to engage with social processes, as opposed to merely chronicling them. This too distinguishes it from the literature of other German-speaking countries. But there are more things uniting the national literatures of the world than there are dividing them, since the great unresolved problems of our century are no longer terri-torially delimited. Wherever we happen to be writing, the threat of the self-destruction of mankind hangs over all of us.

Richard Zipser: *What difference do you see between the GDR literature of the seventies and that of preceding years?*

In the seventies, literature in the GDR became more differentiated. This had begun much earlier and mirrored a similar process in society. Slogan-izing, schematic literature became more and more rare, while many authors began increasingly to emphasize the immediacy of experience. Writers are now giving more honest and direct expression to different formative experiences, with the result that generation gaps appear wider than they did before. Superficial optimism has disappeared from the work of respected authors and new formal elements, such as satire and the use of the utopian and the fantastic as literary devices, both indicate that writers now have a wider knowledge of their society and reflect a courageous and persistent trend towards subjectivity. The basic style of literature has become more critical; apologetics has been shown to be unproductive. A new generation, no longer burdened by our past, is making its mark and it shows a gift for being pleasantly unrestrained. Writers of the middle generation, to which I belong, are trying – though this is by no means easy – to draw up an initial balance-sheet of our lives. And our readers make very clear demands on us: that literature should show life's contradictions, so that they can understand themselves, gain awareness of themselves through literature.

Richard Zipser: *Which contemporary American writers do you read? What is your opinion of them?*

Like so many others, I went through my Hemingway phase, read Salinger and, less intensively, Faulkner. I also found Thomas Wolfe stimulating. Of the more recent American writers, I found Baldwin very interesting and have read Vonnegut and Arthur Miller, as well as Bellow and Capote. I was particularly moved by Carson McCullers and Sylvia Plath. The list is incomplete, of course.

Richard Zipser: *How do you think growing prosperity in society affects literary work?*

Generally, if someone asks you about the dangers increasing affluence poses for intellectual pursuits, they expect a denunciation of the horrors of consumerism. I don't believe, however, that having the daily worry of finding food, clothing and housing can possibly stimulate intellectual interests. The guarantee that these basic needs will be met plays a major part of liberating people to pursue their intellectual concerns. The question needs to be re-phrased. Should the flood of consumer goods, and the fixation, in the advanced industrial nations, of whole sections of the population on consumption, be called 'affluence'? Isn't it rather an example of that phenomenon I referred to earlier, that mankind has let the means that were originally created to meet real needs become ends in themselves – it has allowed control to slip out of its hands? If this is the case, society's desire for literature will also wane and writers will be forced onto the fringes of society.

Richard Zipser: *How are current reading habits in the GDR being influenced by television?*

This question is really related to the previous one. Watching television programmes can have similar consequences to the consumption of material goods, just as it has similar causes. In the GDR, the number of interesting and demanding books published is still very high (so too, incidentally, is the number of detective novels and works of light fiction). More is being read than in Western countries, but there are still families who do nothing but watch television. How far they represent a potential public that could be won over to reading I don't know.

Richard Zipser: *In your opinion, what role should literature play in society today, by comparison with other media?*

Literature should do what other forms of media cannot do. Its role is not to produce sociology, provide information or disseminate ideology, but to articulate a sense of the world and of life which stimulates the reader's individual development, self-discovery and creative desire and helps to develop what is best described in the good old-fashioned word 'personality'. Literature ought not to become one institution among others, but should show the way forward (albeit sceptically) from our threatened existence in the present to a livable future. It should keep us in touch with our roots, promote reason and maturity and keep open a space for those individuals who find themselves hemmed in by all kinds of social constraints. Literature should be a testing ground for experiments which can all too seldom take place in real life and should be the trusty ally of its readers against all possible forms of manipulation.

Richard Zipser: *What do you see as the goal of your work? Is it an attainable one?*

My work has no 'goal'. I can never feel I have reached the end. I would like to be able to express myself fully in what I write so that at the end, nothing – at least nothing that I am able to say – had been left unsaid. That is, of course, impossible.

April 1978

6

I ADMIRE A CERTAIN LACK OF RESTRAINT

A Conversation with Wilfried F. Schoeller*

Wilfried Schoeller: *The question how one as an individual can participate in what we call 'reality' or 'the present', runs like a thread through your work. You have constantly offered new answers. In your novel* The Divided Heaven *(1963), you attempted to raise everyday life to another plane through literature. In so doing, it seems to me that you became more aloof from it.*

Aloof? I'm not sure whether you could call it being aloof. Certainly, I maintain more of a critical distance, but I'm also surer of myself within this reality. You could see this as greater aloofness, increased estrangement, alienation. We should not try to hide the fact that writing always entails an act of elevation to another plane. It is a process of condensing our experiences. In this sense I have not grown more aloof. I experience reality just as keenly as before – perhaps even more keenly in some respects.

Wilfried Schoeller: *Your novel,* The Quest for Christa T. *(1968), concerned an attempt at self-discovery which fails, coming to grief upon reality. In that book, the conflict produced by contact with the outside world seems to have become more intense.*

Yes, definitely more intense. But I'm wary of using words like failure ...

Wilfried Schoeller: *Failure from a dissatisfaction with reality, such as Christa T. experienced.*

*Extract from a TV interview, WDR (Cologne), 9 March 1979. First published in *Süddeutsche Zeitung*, Munich, 10-11 March 1979.

That is a quite central problem for me: what exactly constitutes failure and how do we measure success? I wouldn't like to apply the word 'failure' to Christa T. at all. It is a term often used when this book is being criticized, but that is not the reason I reject it. I tend to measure success and failure by quite different standards from those applied, for example, in the political or economic spheres. Perhaps only literature can do this in our societies, though not to any great effect of course. It is one of the few opportunities available for introducing really new – human – scales of values rather than those taken from economics, politics or other great social institutions of that kind. In this sense, then, Christa T. does not fail by falling short of the self-realization (to use what has become a rather hackneyed term) for which she aims, nor by not managing to get what she wants, nor even by never working out, right up to the end, exactly what it is she does want. For, in spite of these things, in the time allotted to her, she really did live, in the way she was able to and wanted to. I don't know of any other way to define self-realization.

As regards the other question about dissatisfaction with reality, this has certainly become more intense as my own self-awareness has grown, and perhaps as I have been through a greater number of intense experiences. This has not, however, meant retreating from reality – nor could you get that impression from my books. I think I have stood up to reality so far and this is a source of constant tension in my work, but not of weary resignation.

Wilfried Schoeller: *What I am most interested in is this distance between the officially recognized version of reality, with all its demands, and the characters in your work. Having created these characters, have you joined them in distancing yourself from the official pragmatic view?*

Do I distance myself in the same way? I don't really know. You are certainly right that I feel this distance very keenly. I think that certain official descriptions of reality are inaccurate, or at least not accurate enough to mean literature should not attempt a completely different one of its own.

Wilfried Schoeller: *Earlier, in* The Divided Heaven, *this reality was something transient. It had as it were a utopian aura about it . . .*

Yes, that's true . . .

Wilfried Schoeller: *. . . and this, it seems to me, had entirely disappeared by the time* A Model Childhood *was published.*

I don't know whether one can really compare the two books on this count, so it's difficult for me to answer that question.

Wilfried Schoeller: *But I wonder whether one can distinguish a shift away from the utopian.*

May I redirect the question away from my last book, as it really is difficult for me to answer it in that context? Fundamentally, my own – not my characters' – relationship with utopia has, if anything, grown stronger and more certain because reality itself has become more securely established, more stable.

This is a fact: certain structures have become firmly rooted and it is impossible to foresee the possibility of them changing, even if it is desirable that they should, though I leave that open. In any case I see myself confronted by a firmly entrenched reality. For me, only writing can still offer us a chance of bringing in the utopian dimension, an element of hope – I use this unfashionable word unashamedly. This is very important to me. In complete opposition to pragmatism and to the pragmatic demands that are made on literature, I am very concerned, even in my later works, to continue to introduce this utopian element.

Wilfried Schoeller: *Christa T. tried to live according to her wish for a different kind of existence in the world – and I am quoting here from your book. Now a similar tendency is emerging in your society as in ours – the two seem to be sliding inexorably toward each other – for the kind of literature which you have just sketched, that is, intellectual processes which always question the status quo, to be excluded: so that writers are increasingly becoming, as you describe in your book, outsiders.*

I don't deny having felt this sense of being an outsider, nor that exclusion is difficult to overcome. But there is always a reverse side to these experiences.

I cannot compare the situation with that of authors in the West, because I simply don't know enough about it. Here, though, I feel the demand from readers very keenly. I don't claim there are hundreds of thousands of them, but the fact that such an element exists at all in society renews one's sense not only of fulfilling a need but also of being on the outside. Or at least of being part of such a large group of outsiders that the term would no longer apply. In this way, we are not excluded.

Things are becoming polarised. There are now different points of view, and readers are able to choose between them. This is a genuinely positive phenomenon.

Wilfried Schoeller: *Let us try for a moment to look at this from a purely pragmatic political angle. We have the present status quo, to which there is no alternative, and as a result we are seeing perhaps a similar course of political development in the two German states. Those who are trying in their respective states to conceive something beyond that status quo, which increasingly seeks to present itself as an unchangeable and virtually ahistorical order, are either excluded or thrown into the other camp. Hence utopian aspirations strike an increasingly louder note of discord, but the 'outsider' position of utopians also becomes more marked.*

I don't know. I think it is too much to expect to be able to make predictions on this point. There have been so many surprises in the past. I don't see myself as an outsider and don't want to become one. It's possible that I'll be forced to, but it will be against my will and against everything I live and write for. It holds no attraction for me.

On the other hand, the history of German literature, particularly since the beginning of the bourgeois age, shows how literature has repeatedly been excluded and rejected. Then in its next phase of development, the country and the society found they needed the very authors who had been discarded, together with what they had preserved. I cannot be certain that this process will be repeated. Perhaps future generations won't need us at all. Perhaps they won't want history any more, and, if that is the case, then there won't be any. But I simply don't believe that.

I have decided to write as if my work still is, and will remain, of value. This means being very radical – not discordant. Radical and yet with as wide as possible an understanding for others because I can understand why people who lead completely different lives to my own and my fellow-writers' take offence at us. I hope that I will manage to prevent the bridge between normal everyday life, which I respect, and the life which I must lead being torn down.

Wilfried Schoeller: *'The books of today are the deeds of tomorrow', said Heinrich Mann at a time when the Weimar Republic was passing through a difficult period. His words are often quoted in your country. Has the consciousness which you promote through your literature grown?*

I don't think literature has any direct effect on politics. It's a misconception to think that it should. Obviously there are times when writers treating certain subjects in a certain way can influence events. But this is not the situation at the moment. It hasn't been for a long time and won't be for some considerable time to come.

Curiously enough, I am sometimes tempted to argue that literature has no effect at all. But then I end up arguing against myself, on the grounds that this is a misleading way of framing the question. Literature as a whole appears to have no effect. But if it didn't exist, I for one wouldn't wish to be alive at all. To that extent, it must have some effect. It gives me, and I know I am not alone in this, a depth, an extra dimension to life which makes it possible for me to look forward to the next day. In my view, this is the kind of influence which cannot be overestimated – indeed cannot be measured. I wouldn't know what yardstick to apply, what instruments to use.

Wilfried Schoeller: *Let us return once again to the relationship between utopia and literature. If you still maintain, as before, that literature consti-tutes one of the few opportunities for establishing utopia, hasn't literature shifted from being a public arena to a kind of private sanctuary?*

No, I don't see it like that. The public can temporarily abstain from making use of literature. Then literature becomes a kind of vault in which something is stored away to be retrieved later, if desired. But literature is always public, always active and, to my mind, always progressive.

Wilfried Schoeller: *Armed with this idea of being productive, you aim to tackle the contradictions in, and dissatisfaction with, reality. Where do you manage to find the confidence that you have the strength to do that?*

My confidence is by no means consistently high. Quite the contrary. There are periods when I lose not only confidence in myself, but even a certain confidence that what I'm able to contribute is at all relevant to the form of reality which is now emerging. But I am not sure this will be my final word on the matter. I rather think not. Finding the right expression off the top of your head is difficult: you tend to take the first phrase that springs to mind. The first answer that comes to mind here is that I still draw reserves of confidence and creative impulsion from the intensity of my identi-fication with society and from the feeling of being personally affected by everything that affects this society. I can't abstract myself from it. And it is this sense of always being touched by what touches society, although it sometimes drives me to despair, that is the source, amongst other things, of my creative drive. There is still so much that I know and have not yet said. That is a great challenge.

Wilfried Schoeller: *The individual in society, the 'I', is a basic theme of your work. In setting this 'I' up against the prevailing collective self-perception, couldn't you be accused of deviating, creating tension?*

Certainly it causes tensions. I've been aware of that since *Christa T.*, or at least since the reactions to it. I simply have to accept that I create tensions. But I have never seen myself as someone who stands in a completely antagonistic relationship to society, deviating from it, not compromising with it at any price. My opinion is rather that in a society which basically demands productivity (however much it may, in certain periods, reject this) the tension can be fruitful. This is what I try to do with my characters in books like *Christa T.* or *No Place On Earth*. Fundamentally, it is they, the deviants, who are most deeply bound to their time and deviate because they simply cannot conform. They cannot opt for the kind of smooth, untroubled existences they might have led, but which would have been, of course, in a deeper sense, thoroughly useless to their times.

Wilfried Schoeller: *In the GDR there is an extraordinary sense of pride about what has been achieved, if not a sense of complacency, which has no time for utopian aspirations. If literature now takes the form, as you suggest, of a vault in which this utopian element is stored, is it not being pushed more firmly onto the fringes of society today than for example when you wrote* The Divided Heaven *(1963) or* Christa T. *(1968)?*

In our society there are several kinds of pride, including a perfectly justifiable type that is neither arrogance nor haughtiness – and also, admittedly, a certain primitive, superficial pride, which from the outside probably appears distasteful. There is, too, something resembling 'self-examination'. The members of my generation, who are now about fifty years old, have recently begun to look back on their lives and ask, 'What have we actually achieved?' We're talking really about the generation which in the last ten or fifteen years has had most responsibility for what has been done in this country. They are the people who occupy the official positions. Now they are becoming more differentiated and as such, reflect the generally increased degree of differentiation within our society. In our generation, you come across every conceivable position, function and lifestyle. Since all shades of the spectrum are represented and real contradictions exist, far from there being unanimity there are, in my opinion, very sharp conflicts. It is precisely this which provides hope for literature. The fact that so many of us keep this hope alive and do not allow ourselves to be pushed into marginal positions, but hang on to our ideas about society and keep on working at them undeterred, has its roots in this diversity. I think, as a starting point, this is quite productive.

I wouldn't know, for example, what challenges remained in bourgeois society, as regards either new hopes or subject matter. It has really all been said before and there can now only be variations on the same themes. I imagine that if one lived in West Germany one would have to examine the origins of terrorism and the barbaric reaction to it, the causes of this sudden outbreak of barbarism in such a prosperous society. This could certainly still prove stimulating.

We too face heart-rending contradictions which can sometimes appear hopeless. But we always have the possibility of taking up the challenge. I hardly ever feel that a situation is completely unproductive.

Wilfried Schoeller: *Considering the experiences of the last few years, aren't the intellectuals really a vanguard without an army?*

That has often been the case in German history. Perhaps it is currently so in West Germany. From my own experience and what I know from my friends, I would say that it is not the case here. Since we have common, collectively formulated goals, and do not defend any esoteric ideals, a great number of people identify with these ideas. This is because they are not simply objectives we have invented ourselves but are taken from society and the demands it makes on itself.

Wilfried Schoeller: *For you, writing and life are intimately connected. You have expressed this connectedness again and again, but nowhere have I found anything concerning the boundaries, the difference, the distance between the two.*

Probably because it is clear to me that the two are not absolutely identical. So it never occurred to me this was something I should explain. But now you point it out, I see what you mean. I cannot envisage writing and life diverging widely in their basic principles. I cannot imagine an author taking a particular moral position, indeed moralising (which I admit to doing), and yet living in complete opposition to that morality. I see myself constantly trying to bring the two together, though they will never correspond completely.

Apart from this, my life is completely different from my writing. Indeed the hours in which I write are the most concentrated and important part of my life, except for the time I spend with those close to me.

Wilfried Schoeller: *You have had a particular view of writing as an opportunity, so to speak, to get in touch with yourself via your characters. There are not many instances in your work of the author identifying with her characters, but I sense that this is increasing. As too is the harshness of your attitude to yourself.*

The harshness is growing, I am aware of that. The demands I make on myself are growing too, as is the self-criticism. These difficulties all increase when you have been writing a little longer and you're not inclined to take an apologetic view of yourself. I have indeed identified more and more with my characters up to *A Model Childhood*. But that does not mean this same trend will necessarily continue. I'm not completely sure yet, but my future work may well see me identifying with characters that are further from me, and identifying in a more complex way.

Wilfried Schoeller: *Up to now, the major characters in your work have almost exclusively been women.*

That is clearly not by chance. I identify most easily with women. I have become increasingly interested in locating the roots of women's current conflict, their dissatisfaction with life – and this is something I was, of course, concerned with in my short story and my essay about Günderrode. You can see this clearly in the early Romantic period, around 1800, when society, as it came to be shaped by the division of labour, could no longer accommodate the type of person who sought totality, who had a universal conception of happiness. The roots are to be found there.

But I am moving on. I intend in the immediate future to write about men, and I'm already looking forward to it.

Wilfried Schoeller: *For centuries women have been almost completely excluded from literature, in fact from writing. The situation in your society has unquestionably improved. What areas of conflict still remain?*

It is now becoming clear – and in the coming years it will become even clearer – that, quantitively, the contribution of women writers to our literature has increased and will increase further. When I began to write, I was still one of the few women around, and, as a result, I was always on all the committees. That had its advantages and its disadvantages. Nowadays there are many women who see writing as a means of self-realization and some of them are less willing to compromise than men. Recently a woman professor in Poland said to me, 'We women are more inclined to be honest.' The reasons for this lie in history.

The situation for women has improved here in the GDR – even in this field, which, because it has demanded absolute commitment, has always denied women access. But it is obvious that it is a field we can conquer and operate within.

The other part of your question we will probably be able to answer more precisely in five or ten years time. What new sources of conflict may arise? Already friction is mounting. As soon as these women, having naturally exploited the new opportunities gained, begin to question both the nature and the value of the opportunities opened up, they introduce a system of values which does not necessarily square with the one that allowed them to get where they are.

You see, this is a very complex contradiction, and it is one currently being expressed in many works written by women of whom I know a little. I think this is very interesting and differs from what women are writing, for example, in West Germany.

Wilfried Schoeller: *Do you think that, in their lives and their writing, women find it easier to use the first person?*

I look at history to explain why it should be that women in our society relate to one another more naturally, more closely and intimately and with a greater readiness to live out certain values than men. For more than a hundred and fifty years, men have been forced, both by the division of labour and by the patriarchal structure of bourgeois society, to conform and repress themselves. They have fully internalized the values which industrial society has impressed on them. The fact that women were not forced to do this to the same degree both oppressed them further in that they were driven further into the domestic sphere, and yet also reduced the pressure on them to accept these kinds of values completely.

It seems to me – and this is due not to biological but to historical factors – that women are now in a better position to take up new values which they feel to be 'natural' and more human. They simply find this easier to do. This subjective approach too, although immensely difficult for the individual, is becoming easier for them collectively. I am certain that the fashionable tendency for women to build a united front against men will not catch on in the GDR. A time may come when women can help men resolve this question of how we can learn to live together, which concerns a sphere of life that cannot be measured mathematically and where production figures play no part.

Wilfried Schoeller: *Your characters, from Rita in* The Divided Heaven *to Christa T., have all made great demands on society, demands denounced as excessive by those around them. In the character of Günderrode, you also bring out this kind of excessiveness. Has history now moved beyond this theme?*

No not at all. It is simply that the content of the demands has changed – and has done so with each new generation. No one demands what has already been won, such as economic equality, for example. And yet the radicalism of the demands remains and is now being carried into new, more important areas – the really important ones. Mind you, these demands can only be formulated when the others have been met. But I admire a certain lack of restraint and encourage both myself and other women not to temper the excessiveness of their demands but to put those around them to the test – if they are strong enough to do that.

1979

7

ROMANTICISM IN PERSPECTIVE

A Conversation with Frauke Meyer-Gosau*

Christa Wolf: I wrote *No Place on Earth* in 1977. It was a time when I felt impelled to investigate what lay behind failure, and the connection between social despair and failure in literature. Throughout that period, I had a very strong feeling that my back was against the wall and that it was impossible to make any headway. I had to get through a certain period when there seemed to be absolutely no possibility of having any real effect.

1976 represents a turning-point in cultural politics in the GDR, marked outwardly by Biermann[†] losing his citizenship. That led to a polarization among those working in the various cultural fields, especially in literature. It became clear to a group of writers that their direct participation, in a direction they themselves could feel was justified and correct, was no longer required. We were socialists. We were living as socialists in the GDR because we wanted to be involved in that country, make our contribution there. When individuals are thrown back on literature alone, they are plunged into crisis, an existential crisis. It was from that situation, among other things, that my preoccupation with the material of lives like Günderrode's and Kleist's arose. It would have been impossible to tackle the problem with material from the present. The result would have been naturalistic and banal ... insipid.

I chose these two figures in order to play through their problems for myself. I made things very exact historically, both because I couldn't have

*First published in *Alternative*, West Berlin, April-June 1982.
†Wolf Biermann (b. 1936, Hamburg) settled in GDR in 1953 and founded the *Berliner Arbeiter- und Studenten Theater*, which was met with official disapproval. In 1976, whilst on tour in West Germany, he was refused re-entry into the GDR and deprived of GDR citizenship. What became known in the West as the 'Biermann affair' had serious consequences for many GDR authors who signed a public letter of protest against the principle underlying expulsion – Tr.

invented anything as good as the real story, and because I didn't wish to
do violence to the two historical figures. Kleist's letters and Günderrode's
drawings provide so much material on the very question of 'the individual
and society' that I didn't have to 'invent' any characters. Though they are still
invented of course; Günderrode is a rather different person in the essay from
the one in the novel, and today I would see her as someone else again.

These were the compelling motives, then. It was an exercise in self-
understanding and also a form of personal salvation, having had the
carpet pulled out from under me. That was the exact situation. As a
writer, you have the option of working things out in literature – in my
view, people who can't do this have a harder time of it. Rational clarity
wasn't really what bothered me – given time, you can arrive at that by
applying pure thought to specific questions – but I was concerned with the
whole question of where we stand in a particular period and environment,
in the broadest sense and, indeed, in every sense. And, I must also say, in a
concrete historical moment. It's past now. If you survive and keep striving
to be productive, new experiences open up and with them new possibilities, which you didn't see at all before, because you were using a particular experiential grid. A new factor now is the greater threat facing Europe:
this has changed us, created new emphases.

Frauke Meyer-Gosau: *But at that time, five years ago, you particularly
chose the early Romantic period for this step into the past. Apart from the
biographies of Kleist and Günderrode, what interested you in that
period?*

What most interested me was to investigate when this dreadful split
between individuals and society had really begun. At what point did the
division of labour take hold of people to such a degree that literature came
to be expelled from the realm that society, in its self-understanding,
decreed to be the important, essential one, or, indeed, regarded as reality?
At the same time, the feminine element was also being expelled from
society, though this had begun much earlier. In industrial society, the
'feminine element' is as little present as the 'intellectual element': neither
women nor intellectuals have any influence on the key processes determining our lives. It was the severity of this transformation into an
outsider, which I felt within my own self existentially, that I wanted to
examine, not least, of course, in order to distance myself from it.

Where and when did it begin? In the writings and lives of the Romantics you find an abundance of documentation on this; they perceived with
some sensitivity that they were outsiders, that they were not needed in a
society which was in the process of becoming industrial society, of intensi-
fying the division of labour, of turning people into appendages of

machines. At the same time, it was also a society that was re-casting the concept of 'Progress' in a way that broke with the Enlightenment defini-tion – and this was being done by the very same people who would not be reading the books of 'writers'. Though more people were learning to read and there were more schools, the texts they read or were allowed to read – or in fact were able to read – were not of course the texts of these authors. Though none of these developments really seem so explosive, the Roman-tics were enormously sensitive to them. The fact that we really can detect similarities here to our own reactions to processes and phenomena of a quite different order of seriousness, prompted me to take this so-called step into the past.

Frauke Meyer-Gosau: *From what you say, Romanticism as a literary movement was of no great concern to you?*

The concept of 'Romanticism' played no role whatever in my thinking. At no point did I think to myself that I was working on Romanticism. Neither Günderrode nor Kleist is, in the narrower sense, a Romantic. What inter-ested me was something different; I wondered why it was that after the Classical generation such a host of young authors emerged, who mani-festly could not 'cope' with their times, with their talent, with literature and with their personal lives. Who, in bourgeois terms and also in the view of a particular current in Marxist literary theory, 'failed'. I should perhaps also mention that there was the discussion between Anna Seghers and Georg Lukács in 1938-9 – in the letters they exchanged between Paris and Moscow in the years of emigration, after the great Expressionism Debate. Lukács was at that time entirely committed to classical aesthetics and sought the same perfection in modern art. For him, the great, classical, bourgeois novel was, in fact, the yardstick of all art. Seghers took a differ-ent view and, as proof that the times were themselves opposed to the arts, adduced this string of names of writers who had either lived after the classical writers or whose lives had partially overlapped with them, and who had not attained this classical perfection, which involves abstinence and renunciation. The list included such names as Lenz, Kleist, Günder-rode, Grabbe, Büchner and Hölderlin. Günderrode was the one name I did not know. From that point on, I began to collect anything I could about her. Then I read in a literary history that Kleist and Günderrode were said to have met, 'on the Rhine', at the beginning of the new century. From accounts of both lives, I deduced when this could have occurred: 1804. I imagined that they met in Winkel. This has not been proved, but it needs no proof. For my part, I'm convinced the meeting didn't actually take place. But this was just the external pretext, not my inner motive, which, as I've already explained, was, as ever, autobiographical in nature.

What came increasingly to interest me, when I began to work on it, was their – the Romantics' – attempt at an experiment in living. I didn't see this merely as a literary question – that wasn't the dominant aspect any more – but I was concerned with what these young people, as they then were, had been trying to do: living in groups and, since they found living in society wasn't possible, living on the margins of society – though from a literary point of view, they were at its centre. This is the remarkable thing about them: while they lived out their various experiments on the fringes of bourgeois society, they were nonetheless central as literary figures. The way they did that, the way they carried it through, and the way that the *women* initiated it all, since it was they who needed it the most – the way they stuck to it through all the colossal social and personal conflicts and all kinds of material difficulties – that was what fascinated me. In my mind, this all came, in fact, to be fused together in the concept of 'Romanticism', a concept which came to have a quite different meaning for me. For me it now has nothing to do with all the things it meant when I was studying German literature and which many today perhaps still see in it – moon and June Romanticism, lovers' trials and tribulations, heartaches, a romanticized view of the Middle Ages, clericalism. I now see early Romanticism as a social experiment by a small, progressive group which subsequently, when society has responded in a totalitarian and negative, or at any rate a restrictive, manner, broke apart under the strain and withdrew in various different directions. There then arose a whole host of things: clericalism, nostalgia for the Middle Ages or whatever you will. But there was a time when the movement was progressive, and that interested me.

Frauke Meyer-Gosau: *Once again, within this group, it was the women writers who were particularly important to you. . . .*

Yes, as I later became aware, I unconsciously enjoyed watching a production process like Günderrode's; for me, it was a kind of self-regeneration. The way she created was so thoroughly pure, with never a thought of an audience, free of any expectation. Yet this – and this was the other side of the coin – also killed her, since she found no audience. But, seen from today's point of view, this was ultimately a therapeutic, unadulterated process of self-expression. She thought only of herself, though she did so in the best sense of thinking of the theme of her work without experiencing herself as part of its object. She was always a subject. This is also part of my own motivation in dealing with these figures: the attempt to get at the dammed-up sources of productivity.

Working on Günderrode and Bettine was very refreshing. In spite of all the heavy, depressing elements in Günderrode, which also came to weigh upon me, my reaction was principally one of astonishment at how this young woman expressed herself in a manner so completely free of influence, except for the demands she made on herself. And Bettine as a foil to her, for whom I also felt great sympathy and respect on account of the joviality, directness and indeed courage she showed both in her life generally and, particularly, in her politics later in Berlin. The way she openly said what she was thinking, when she poured out her feelings in her letters to her various admirers to the point of triviality, sentimentality and making herself ridiculous; this touched me greatly and I also found it admirable.

We're now coming to the heart of the motives and experiences which, irrespective of present circumstances, led me to write *No Place* and the two essays. In my experience, the choices before us are collapsing one after another so that life offers fewer and fewer real alternatives. This might be the philosophical correlative of the title *No Place on Earth*. To avoid any misunderstanding, I should say that my life is basically structured by contradictions: that's not something I find negative – nor ever have. But it can be uncomfortable, and also extremely irritating. It can bring one's whole existence into question. Yet if those contradictions contain impulses from both sides towards resolution, they are not shattering or lethal. It seems to me at the moment that there are increasingly fewer of these productive contradictions, while the number of unproductive contradictions and unlivable alternatives is on the increase. It's precisely this that makes so many people anxious: the fact that they feel they're being hemmed in.

Frauke Meyer-Gosau: *The motivations that cause you to write, or that play a part in your writing are one thing, but when it comes to publication, other programmatic intentions come into play. In the Günderrode essay, for example, you write that it was high time the existing assessments of the Romantics were taken to task.*

Literary studies in the GDR had begun to make the same re-adjustments at the same time or some time before. It is now virtually free of these taboos about Romanticism. The quotation that is often heard, which comes, sadly, from Goethe: 'I call the Classical the healthy, the Romantic the sick', is now at last no longer taken as the last word on Romanticism. On the other hand, one cannot cover up or ignore developments within the Romantic movement which were potentially negative – and which were also in some respects translated into reality. That I freely admit. For example, I have just been reading a letter from Rahel Varnhagen, which she wrote in 1819 around the time of the Karlsbad Decrees, about the attacks on Jewish citizens which were breaking out quite suddenly in a great number of towns. These didn't lead to direct persecution in the form of pogroms, but they did involve vulgar abuse and social discrimination. Amongst others, she names Achim von Arnim and Clemens Brentano as the intellectual instigators and describes how an atmosphere gradually arose out of 'intellectual' anti-Semitic tendencies, which incited the mob, as they put it at the time, to 'mob-like' excesses. All this did happen and cannot be forgotten or swept under the carpet.

Frauke Meyer-Gosau: *Initially, however, the authors you're talking about saw themselves as a socially progressive movement and acted as such?*

Acted? Not all of them. Few of them got as far as action. The fact that their ideals did imply practical consequences is clear, particularly in Bettine's writing. She maintained an interest in the possibilities for direct political action right into her old age, when she again became free of household duties. But she is almost an exception. The basic formative experience of this generation was that they never managed to translate into political reality the lofty expectations which the French Revolution had unleashed; indeed they did not even dare hope they might. At least, we must add, in Germany. Many became resigned when no reforms followed the wars of liberation of 1813-15. It isn't so fantastically remarkable, after all, that people should collapse or break down as a result of the discrepancy between their strong, practical, day-to-day political demands and the opportunities society offered, or that they should learn to lie low and adapt to that discrepancy – for all of which they are then criticized. It would be remarkable if things were any different. And what a loss it would be if nothing remained of this group of people, who at least tried to stretch themselves to the limit.

Frauke Meyer-Gosau: *Once again, women had more constraints to overcome than men.*

Yes. In early Romanticism, in Jena and Heidelberg, the images of men and women came somewhat closer together. A new concept of culture emerged. Within these groups, women were able to find roles for themselves more freely – at least insofar as their intellectual and spiritual attitudes were concerned.

That they still had a hard time of it, looked at from an external viewpoint, is certainly the case. You only have to think of the fate of Caroline Schlegel-Schelling. Or, to take another case, Günderrode, who had to live in a convent home without any prospect of creating her own life. She was materially dependent and, not being married, was unable to play any kind of role at all in public life or to make a living for herself, and there was no man there to earn money for her.

Frauke Meyer-Gosau: *Nevertheless, though the programme for changing their own lives was radical enough, the women writers were not so radical themselves as to dare to publish under their own names.*

This can perhaps only be understood if you have a feel for the atmosphere of the period. Certain things we hold back from doing today, shortcomings we are sometimes even partially conscious of, will, I am sure, not be understood in years to come; not even if we describe them directly, since many taboos cannot be understood as an effect of explicit prohibitions, but only as the result of the whole nature and mood of the times and the limitations within oneself – as a mixture in fact of both these things. And that, I think, is how it must have been for these women who had massive external limitations to cope with, and who were always too poor, who always had too little money. Like Bettine, for example, who bore a child almost every year of her marriage and who, given those circumstances, obviously could not – or didn't even have the inclination to – do anything. During that time, she was constantly absorbed by the cares of the nursery and the household and she complained greatly of how the other part of her had been completely repressed and stifled, browbeaten into angry submission. Then she broke out again and, in the end, became quite radical. You could see the behaviour of each of these women as a result of their circumstances, though their temperament and character also played a role. Taken together, they perhaps give us a picture of the times; how the times weighed down on each individual, in spite of their differences.

Take Günderrode for example. Why did she publish under a male pseudonym? She was a shy, timorous person and, as the eldest daughter of a poor noble family, she would have to have been. She was certainly not a pushy, radical type. She was more of a radical in her writing than her life. In many other women, the opposite was the case. Dorothea Schlegel was more radical in her life than in her writing. As for women publishing under their own names, that occurred in some individual cases in the nineteenth century, but it did not become standard practice until this century. Even today, as I am constantly hearing, woman have to wrestle with this problem more than men, since they very often open up as persons when they write, and in this sense become 'recognizable'. You can also see in their reactions to criticism that they are apparently more vulnerable. This is perhaps historically determined. . . .

Frauke Meyer-Gosau: *Yet Günderrode and Bettine, different as they were in both their writing and their lives, did publish.*

It seems to have been the case with Günderrode that she was someone who obeyed the rules. For example, she conformed more closely to the prevailing aesthetic canon, which is a very important matter when you are writing: to submit completely to this specific aesthetic, to recognize it as the highest law, by which you judge and can yourself be judged.

And in that age, art was what classicism had decreed that it was. Furthermore, Günderrode was extraordinarily vulnerable on account of the impossibility of belonging to the man she had fallen in love with, I would be tempted to say, by accident. This alone would have represented 'success' for her and would have allowed her to feel she had transcended the banality and restriction of her times, which is what everyone who writes longs to do. That is clearly why one writes.

Things were different with Bettine. Working on her, I came upon an almost monstrous, extravagant, untrammelled epistolary literature, which cared not one iota for judgments of artistic merit. That was an amusing, exhilarating discovery. And her extensive social activity too, which even included direct social studies among the poor in Berlin's 'Vogtland'. In fact there wasn't much she didn't do. She burst right through all the restrictions placed upon her and did not use the harshness of the times as an excuse for laziness or cowardice.

Frauke Meyer-Gosau: *The question remains, however, what it is about these Romantics and the picture you draw of them that so interests today's readers?*

Right. They were, perhaps, one of the first generations to be inwardly torn by a sense that the potentialities which they felt very keenly, very vividly within themselves, which they could test out in conversations and literary endeavours, could not be realized in action. This is, it seems to me, an experience shared again today by young people in particular, for though they don't usually have to contend with the difficult material worries that used to exist, they still want to live what they feel to be a really human life, and to do so not in a self-centred way, but in a way that is open and shared with others. To this extent, we are not unlike people in the West. As a result, we can see groups of friends developing and discover – with all the conflicts this entails – what it is like to try and live together when you make an effort to be honest with one another, when you try to develop a creativity which, though it may involve creating pottery or clothes or whatever, does not have material goods alone as its sole end-result; or when you try to bring up children together. Naturally, in industrial societies, which are geared to efficiency and mass production, this remains a marginal phenomenon. We should have no illusions about this. But, nonetheless, culture is what is lived. And this, I believe, is what attracts young people today.

Frauke Meyer-Gosau: *The Romantics' experiments in living came to nothing. Might not the failure of their ambitious plans find an echo in the apocalyptic feelings of many contemporary readers?*

Often at readings, though not in fact so much in letters, I am asked why I chose a subject from so far back in history. And also, to put it bluntly, why I chose so sad a theme, these people who later committed suicide. I find the question quite legitimate.

There is a form of reaction – and I have had this with all my books – whereby readers think that if someone dies in the book (in *Christa T.* or with these two, Kleist and Günderrode), this somehow reflects my own feelings. That there are people who draw such over-hasty conclusions can perhaps be blamed in part on our literary criticism – and probably on literary criticism in both German states – which sees the intentions of the author as necessarily coincident with the fates of her or his characters. I can tell you there are many readers who realize that, even though my questions cut ever more deeply into the wounds of our time – and, hence, into my own wounds – I'm not planning to throw in the towel.

Frauke Meyer-Gosau: *Doesn't a title like* No Place on Earth *also invite readers to identify themselves negatively?*

When the title occurred to me ... I can remember that I drew back at the time from its radical ring. But then I felt it was right, right for my experience. Later I noticed that it obviously expressed a general experience. I wasn't aware of that at the time and even if I had been, I wouldn't have chosen any other title.

Since *The Quest for Christa T.* appeared, I have realised there are some readers who take this particular kind of literature, which they believe they understand, as something to be 'celebrated'. They don't see it as a challenge or a provocation, but as a consecration of a momentary state of being, in which they would like to fix themselves. Yet this is not at all the way the author sees things. She regards what she writes as a transitory moment of stasis within a broader process. I would not have been able to write a book the same way at some other point in time. So, on occasion, I get a kind of eerie feeling when I am faced with strong reactions to a book years later and I can hardly remember exactly where I stood on things when I wrote it. I do, however, also know readers who treat books as invitations to do some work of their own, who are not simply consumers; these readers are almost like collaborators in my writing. The letters they send are essential to me; not only because they provide an echo for my work, but because they put something of themselves into it. So the echo that comes back is a powerful one.

Frauke Meyer-Gosau: *I also think the fact that in* No Place on Earth *you adapted your style and tone so closely to Romanticism's own had an effect on how the book was received. By contrast, a book like* A Model Childhood *by its very construction immediately causes the reader to adopt a different stance. . . .*

It's true that there's a lot of quoted material in *No Place on Earth.* But it is my voice that's speaking. I have adapted my style, but I consider that quite legitimate.

My method in *A Model Childhood* was different and it produced a different effect. Older readers remembered their own childhood or experiences from the period of fascism and then often spoke about this for the first time, on many occasions trembling with emotion. For younger readers, the book also satisfied a need for information, a need which to some extent they were not so conscious of. Real needs were met, and that was part of my intention, as it was in the essays on Günderrode and Bettine.

Frauke Meyer-Gosau: *And in* No Place on Earth *there is the musical lilting tone.*

Someone told me recently that they felt it sensually, in pictures. I made several starts before I found the right 'inner tone'. There was a certain chord inside me, just waiting to be plucked, through this particular type of diction. Because really it was more a matter of diction than writing, at least at the beginning. I was also trying to get at a certain evocative power of speech, a particular rhythm. This was something different from most of *A Model Childhood,* which contained more analysis, a lot of documentary material. And I saw it as having a different function.

Frauke Meyer-Gosau: *I imagine reactions to* No Place on Earth *must have differed in the Federal Republic from those in the GDR – the reader's current social context is surely quite different.*

Sometimes I try an experiment. I read readers' letters without looking at the envelope to see where they have come from. When I do that, I can't always tell whether the letter has come from the Federal Republic or the GDR. In fact I would say it's almost a general rule that I can't distinguish them. Clearly they have similar needs, which the texts concern themselves with. The letters are also often from similar people – I get to know them at readings. It's a similar type of person, which is neither an East nor a West German, neither a GDR nor a Federal Republic type. But it's a type of – usually young – person, who has quite precise expectations, which are not 'shared'.

Frauke Meyer-Gosau: *Two social systems so different from one another and yet the same sense that something's missing?*

What's present in the life of both is a stern draught of no-nonsense realism, in the sense that something's only officially acknowledged as 'real' if it is institutionalized in some form or other. Both states are institutionalized. In both, those wholly tangible aspirations that can be satisfied by institutions have been institutionalized. This process has gone well in both states. Much of it concerns what is crucial for everyday, material life, even what is essential for social existence in general, insofar as certain communicative needs simply must be satisfied. These structures have been formed. They exist. They function. Basically, everything that institutions can conceive of has been covered. And yet it's a fact, all the same, that institutions can't deal with the essential things. These slip through the perfect structures, and this is something that people – particularly the generations younger than my own – are now seeing. 'There must be more to it than this', said Volker Braun once. The 'really important things in life', as they would say, cannot be satisfied by all the welfare provision that exists in the two states. By this, I mean the need for . . . poetry in one's life. For everything that can't simply be counted or measured, or put in statistical terms. And here literature has its role as a means of self-assertion. I have often seen it playing this role and I'm very sympathetic to the idea. Literature as a means of self-assertion, self-confirmation and therefore as a vehicle of desire. And here we're back on the path that takes us straight to Romanticism again. . . .

Frauke Meyer-Gosau: *From what you say, it seems that my assumption that GDR readers must read your texts differently from those in the Federal Republic is wrong?*

From my own experience or my observation of readers' attitudes, I can't see that the territorial division you're referring to, a division determined by the social order, by differences of social setting, political state or economic system, really exists in literature. It seems to me that literature gives expression to things that can't be confined to a particular territory or society. Many people share quite similar experiences. If you stand at a machine for eight and a half hours a day, you're bound to react in a very particular way. There is a basic pattern which gets imprinted upon people. We live in modern industrial societies, in patriarchal societies which are hierarchically organized. As a consequence, these societies possess similar features. Against the background of this basic situation, literature must also express similar conflicts, alongside the differences that do exist. I don't deny there are differences – in fact I find them interesting. First of all, though, we shouldn't be all that amazed by the fact that the literature of one part of the country is understood in the other, when in fact there are clear possibilities for identifying with it.

Frauke Meyer-Gosau: *I'd still like to maintain my other hypothesis, though, my theory that women's reactions to* No Place on Earth *are different from men's.*

Overall, I get more letters from women than from men. Recently at a reading in Hamburg, at the end of a discussion with very large group – 450 people – a male participant asked me, 'Is it always like this at your readings? Is it always only the women who speak?' It wasn't until that point that I actually became conscious myself that a great number of women had spoken that evening. Generally, in meetings and discussions men talk much more. There seems to be something here, then, that prompts women to speak. Women perhaps feel directly concerned. Perhaps men have to build up a certain reserve and defence against certain emotions.

Frauke Meyer-Gosau: *How does this defence manifest itself?*

I've heard comments like, 'She must be crazy – clinically insane – to write things like that.' Comments from men, deeply defensive. I often hear that, though it's not so often said to my face or written directly; I find it in many critics; I find it in ideological debates.

Frauke Meyer-Gosau: *What are they defending themselves against?*

Against the entire world-view that underlies what I write. In 'world-view' here, I also include the sense of 'view of society'. I start out from the fact that we live in a male society, that we have for centuries been living in a male culture and that this has had tremendous consequences, the ultimate one being that all of us now, men and women together, live on the verge of annihilation. Such conclusions are easily dismissed as too sweeping, as 'feminine' (and therefore extravagant), so they can be disregarded. This is what the male defence is directed against: I'm over-the-top, pretentious, too emotional, or else too sad, or too complicated. I'm not arguing that my works shouldn't be criticized. But when criticism is always massively focused on the same aspects of my work and I can't and won't give these up, then we're simply talking about genuine differences of opinion, which are often not expressed as such, but disguised as literary criticism. But this is such a common occurrence and almost every author knows it well. There's really nothing more to be said about it.

Frauke Meyer-Gosau: *Men's defensive reactions aren't directed against the androgynous features, then, for example in the figure of Kleist in* No Place on Earth?

They are sometimes directed against Kleist's 'effeminate' traits! Recently someone said to me that Kleist was the author of Michael Kohlhaas, a sturdy, spirited writer of great verve, and I had deformed him by giving him effeminate characteristics.

Frauke Meyer-Gosau: *That would be the male reader's fear, then, having his femininity found out?*

I don't know if I'd say 'his femininity'. That's perhaps too sweeping a way of putting it. I believe, rather, that it's a diffuse sense of unease about anything hybrid, about fluid transitions, about things not being simply one thing or the other: friend or foe, male or female; a fear of learning to live with rather than against one another; not in fixed antinomies, but in fluid transitions, in productive alternatives which don't need to be destructive. We haven't learnt this yet. We haven't been educated for it. It's having to face up to this that causes fear.

Winter 1982

8

FROM A DISCUSSION AT OHIO STATE UNIVERSITY

A Conversation with Christa and Gerhard Wolf*

Henry Schmidt: *We would like to know how you influence, how you complement each other. When did you begin to work together?*

Christa Wolf: We got to know each other as early as 1949 when we were still students. We both began studying education and then transferred to German Studies. Gerhard's literary influence on me really came via poetry. With Rilke, to begin with ...

Gerhard Wolf: The Cassandra poems too.

Christa Wolf: The ones you wrote?

Gerhard Wolf: Yes.

Christa Wolf: I think Gerhard's influence on my work is really greater than mine on his. When I am writing something, we discuss it a lot beforehand. To begin with, talking about it gradually brings me to a better understanding of what I'm trying to do. His reactions bring me nearer and nearer to what I'm trying to achieve, because he is very aware of what that is. When I finish something, he is, naturally, the first to read it. My younger daughter, who is training to be a theatre director, once wrote a sketch about the family, called 'Father reads mother's manuscript, mother reads father's – what's the difference?'. She showed how he becomes completely engrossed in what he is doing and subjects mother's manuscript to his stern critical eye, as if it were his own. How he, as it were, beats me about the head with his criticisms and tears it to pieces. When he

*First published in German in *The German Quarterly* (Ohio), no. 1, 1984.

has finished, I say, 'What on earth shall I do, it's completely dreadful!', and he says, 'Why do you say that, it's very good ... there are just these one or two minor points on each page.' And then the other way round. I am reading his manuscript, sitting in the chair, reading silently, not saying a word. He paces round me like a tiger or goes into his room, then comes back after just a few minutes and looks over my shoulder. My approach is quite different: I go about things calmly and carefully. He has more to say about my work than I do about his. I get more out of it. These are as it were, our mental profiles.

Henry Schmidt: *Can we hear Gerhard's side of that?*

Gerhard Wolf: I'm so used to being an editor and I admire literature so much that I am too inhibited to write, to write fiction that is. This has become an almost insurmountable block.

Christa Wolf: You really have to be a touch mad to write.

Gerhard Wolf: I'm good at getting inside someone else's text, I think.

Christa Wolf: He does this with other people's writing as well, not just mine. And he has often made it physically possible for me to write too, by doing much of what a woman, who is married with two children, is traditionally obliged to do.

Helen Fehervary: *I believe initially you were both working as critics?*

Christa Wolf: Yes, I wrote criticism – in the bad sense of the word – as the kind of critic who judges books by predetermined criteria. But that horrified me so much that I gave it up.

Helen Fehervary: *But, even then, you had the feeling that you had to find an alternative mode of expression?*

Christa Wolf: Yes, I felt I had somehow to express myself differently. But I think the German course, which we both took, set me back years.

Gerhard Wolf: We completely absorbed Lukács's theories.

Christa Wolf: The dogmatic nature of German literary theory at the time, and of Marxist philosophy – I have to include that as well – delayed the start of my writing career by years. They robbed me of the immediacy of my experience. This only really broke through again in *Christa T..* The first traces appeared in *The Divided Heaven*, but the real breakthrough, the moment the dams burst, came in *Christa T.*

Gerhard Wolf: I have always found the connection between author and work very interesting. But I suppressed that interest for a long time. I wrote the standard type of criticism, until the truly creative dimension of literary work came to interest me so much that I broke away from conventional criticism.

Christa Wolf: I worked first of all in the Writers' Union, in the young writers' department, then I became an editor on *Neue Deutsche Literatur (New German Literature)*. After that, I spent a year as an editor for the Neues Leben (New Life) publishing house. Throughout this period we were both, in our own way, dealing with young writers, whose manuscripts we had to judge. They were constantly hovering around us. You always had to hold your own on the political battlefield, and sometimes fend off fierce political criticism. This created a sense of solidarity between us, though that doesn't mean we formed an alliance against the outside world.

Helen Fehervary: *To us, this seems a really enviable process. In the West, we are compelled to make our way individually. Here you either work completely alone or in a 'team'. The way you obviously complement one another in your relationship perhaps represents a third way.*

Christa Wolf: Well, it's really just fortunate that things have turned out this way.

Gerhard Wolf: It isn't unusual.

Christa Wolf: It shouldn't be unusual, we don't really feel it's strange. But I would find it difficult to imagine myself in a job without Gerhard being there. I would feel a lot less sure of myself. When I have finished a manuscript, his opinion gives me a sense of security. I never let it go before he says, 'Yes, that's alright for others to see.'

Henry Schmidt: *To what extent is literary criticism useful, how useful can it ever be? Twenty years ago, Christa, you commented that it tends to be written with an eye towards higher authorities and that critics are always having to prove themselves as critics. Are there critics from whom you have learned a lot? Is there a style of critical discourse with which you feel you could enter into a dialogue?*

Gerhard Wolf: I think this is possible if the criticism in fact turns into what, in the best sense of the word, could be called essay writing, when the author brings his or her own concerns into play. A good example would be Hans Mayer's *Aussenseiter (Outsiders)*, in which he tries for the first time to explain his – previously concealed – outlook on life by reference to exemplary characters. Unlike his other books, for example, in which he sets out to discuss Thomas Mann, here he goes beyond the role of literary critic he has consciously performed elsewhere.

Christa Wolf: I think that pure literary criticism is often a mistake. Critics treat a book as if it were an object, just as natural scientists handle an object in an experiment. But this is precisely the kind of scientific approach which is decidedly inapplicable to literature. If critics cannot bring themselves to relate their own observations to the subjectivity expressed in the book, if they can't openly adopt a position on it, then their criticism will always be constricted. It was in the reviews of *Cassandra* that I noticed this very clearly. Some critics try to hide behind a pseudo-objectivity, but their own personal inhibitions as people and as literary critics are so obvious in every line they write that one is forced to laugh.

Gerhard Wolf: Literary theorists don't deliberately aggravate the situation.

Christa Wolf: They do try to be fair.

Gerhard Wolf: But they don't express many ideas of their own. There is, rather, a whole tissue ...

Christa Wolf: ... of quotations. ...

Gerhard Wolf: Their own position is rarely clear.

Christa Wolf: This doesn't mean, though, that literary theorists can't teach me anything. There are literary theorists in this country, with whom I am in contact, who immerse themselves in an author without getting carried away in their praise of them.

Gerhard Wolf: Our critics are constantly under pressure, consciously or unconsciously, to proclaim solemn ideological allegiances.

Henry Schmidt: *Isn't this because literary criticism is under institutional pressures? It constantly has to prove itself either as journalism or as literary theory. Critics always have to keep one eye on the institution.*

Christa Wolf: Yes, of course, that's exactly how it is.

Gerhard Wolf: Or else the critics have internalized the institutional demands. I don't want to suggest that they are being dishonest. They are genuinely convinced these are justified.

Christa Wolf: It's not that they are hypocrites. But it is the ones with conviction who are the worst. Those who are convinced that it is right to use a book as a means to an end, to prove either themselves or some ideological or literary concept correct, cannot be persuaded otherwise. Here, the author's only course is to keep well out of it all.

Susanne Pongratz: *If the writer's tone is a personal one, their work becomes much more difficult to evaluate.*

Christa Wolf: Of course, so judgements will vary.

Helen Fehervary: *The highest priority for me is not that I interpret your story 'perfectly' but that I myself participate in the process that you are going through. I rediscover myself in this process. I am working with you. I am trying to think with you. In effect it is a conversation. I want to take up the half woven fabric of the text . . .*

Christa Wolf: . . . and send the shuttle across again, add another row. That is really a way of working together, and I find it much more stimulating than this continual judgmentalism.

Gerhard Wolf: *For their part, the astute critics who are aware of this conflict now find themselves in a tricky situation. They don't want to discredit the author. It's not a good idea to say what an author in a particular situation is attacking . . .*

Christa Wolf: . . . or avoiding . . .

Gerhard Wolf: . . . or what sources he or she is drawing on, because they might be taboo.

Helen Fehervary: *Where do you draw the boundary between criticism and literature? Could one call the essays in the Frankfurt lectures criticism? When I write an epilogue to an Ingeborg Bachmann book, for example, that is closer to criticism. It had been expected that the Frankfurt lectures would be nearer to poetics, which was obviously impossible too. I don't write criticism any more. I'm not saying that criticism serves no purpose, quite the reverse. I would like to imagine criticism attempting, not to defame the author, but honestly to mediate between author and reader (which also includes criticism in the narrower sense of the word).*

Gerhard Wolf: Like Benjamin's commentary on Brecht's poems, for example, where the commentator brings out three or four dimensions – these are truly great interpretations.

Christa Wolf: A contrasting example would be Lukács's readings of Kleist, which take Kleist out of a very specific historical context, and make him a precursor of irrationalism and thus of fascism.

Helen Fehervary: *Lukács objectifies Kleist, whereas, with Benjamin, one senses rather that he shares the same problematic. He is working alongside Brecht on the same questions.*

Henry Schmidt: *Lukács approaches the matter in an* a priori *way. He knows beforehand exactly what he wants to prove. In the Kleist critique, you can see how this simply works itself out in the process of writing.*

Gerhard Wolf: Lukács has a set of fixed aesthetic rules in his head and he judges each item by the degree to which it corresponds – or fails to correspond – to this aesthetic.

Helen Fehervary: *And Lukács as subject always remains intact.*

Christa Wolf: Yes, he never really stops playing the teacher.

Helen Fehervary: *You think then that, as critics, we should not treat writers as if they were beneath us – or, indeed, above us?*

Christa Wolf: That's right, more as equals. The ideal relationship between a critic and an author would be some kind of congeniality, although this will probably only very rarely be achieved in practice. I find a certain honesty in a critic who says that this book or play made a great impression on me, or left me cold, rather than saying that a poem like this must make this or that impression on everybody. That is dishonest. To clarify what I mean here, I had an epilogue to Kleist's *Penthesilea* to write, and I was suddenly able to connect this in with my preliminary research for *Cassandra.* That way, I hit upon reasons why Kleist had chosen to express his problems in the character of a woman, which is very different, for instance, from the way he proceeded in *Prince Friedrich of Homburg.* I am always interested in the subject behind the written text.

Helen Fehervary: *I would never try, with any book, though, to draw out the personal motivations of a living author. I think that is barbaric, voyeuristic, cannibalistic.*

Christa Wolf: Yes, I approve of such discretion and I would apply it to past authors too. In the *Penthesilea* essay I approach this question directly: should we now feel free to rake over Kleist's personal history and express in so many words what he so carefully tried to conceal in *Penthesilea*? This applies to my work on the character of Cassandra too. Studying early civilisation, I was shocked to discover that in our culture women have had no voice for three thousand years. Now I have taken up the first voice to be handed down to us, and have tried to scrape the overlay of male mythology from it: the myth that she was a seer who was not believed because the god Apollo had divested her of all credibility. I asked myself what it really must have been like in the social conditions in which such a woman could live – and certainly did live. That was my work of demythologization: to analyze the syndrome of alienation which patriarchy has inflicted upon every female voice in this culture. So I am reconstituting a character based on my own experience that in our present civilisation every woman, when she tries to become active within existing institutions, is turned into an object. As to whether this situation can be alleviated, or whether a solution can be found, these are the central questions occupying me at the current stage in my life. I have now got to the point where I can pose these questions without being overwhelmed by them because they are beyond my grasp. They constitute the internal 'plot' of the book on Cassandra, though at the same time it was very important for me to make her historically as 'real' as possible – as far as I could imagine her. As with Kleist and Günderrode, I did not want to do her violence in any way.

Gerhard Wolf: In the GDR today there is a much greater awareness of tradition than in West Germany. Our lyricists look much more consciously and directly to Klopstock and Hölderlin. In our *Markischen Dichtergarten*, for example, in the issues edited by Ewald von Kleist, Anna Louisa Karschin and F.W.A. Schmidt, Günter de Bruyn and myself try to give a new lease of life to a literary tradition which has been submerged, and in some cases almost forgotten.

Helen Fehervary: *Which tradition do you mean?*

Gerhard Wolf: Its origins lie in literary currents and undeveloped movements that existed in Prussia but never produced truly great literary works. Our classical period is really a pyramid, and we know only its summit –

Goethe and Schiller. Beneath them there is an incredibly wide variety of currents which reach forward into the current literature of the GDR.

Henry Schmidt: *That seems to be an extension of Brecht's concept of tradition, a popular tradition which Brecht himself did not recognise or even rejected, wouldn't you agree?*

Christa Wolf: These efforts are no longer conceived in a particular relation to Brecht, not even a contradictory relation. It used to be the case that everything produced in the GDR in the way of literature or the appraisal of literature had its roots in Brecht or Seghers or Becher or Lukács, but in recent times that has changed. East German literature has developed its own traditions.

Helen Fehervary: *On that point, Western scholars of German literature have repeatedly suggested that the GDR literature of the seventies is characterised by a 'new subjectivity', a term that is often employed in an ahistoric and apolitical way.*

Gerhard Wolf: Yes, so here one must describe exactly what this subjectivity means to the individual as he or she begins to use the subjective 'I' again. Like, for example, Volker Braun who suddenly quite deliberately replaced his usual collective 'we' with 'I'.

Christa Wolf: Heiner Müller, too, said 'One can no longer write without bringing oneself in as the author'. The reasons why this happened at this particular point in time are historical. It was not done against history; it is, rather, one more way to approach history and to tackle the problem it poses.

Gerhard Wolf: For East German writers, this subjectivism cannot be understood as individualism because the social context is all-powerful. It is high time that the relationship between the individual and society was defined once and for all. So one tries to find some sure ground by looking to the past. To Bobrowski's famous line, for example, 'How must the world be constituted for a moral being?' We didn't know where this statement came from. In fact it is from Hölderlin's *Systemprogramm*, which he wrote with Schelling and Hegel.

Christa Wolf: Bobrowski took this theme up and others came to it through him. This takes us right back to the beginning of the nineteenth century. References of this kind are always so insistently present that when one takes up a text, one always has a whole intricate network in one's hand.

Helen Fehervary: *Right now in the West, there is an anti-Enlightenment trend. New tendencies in East German literature are frequently called upon to legitimate this tendency. But in order to understand and describe the political development of women, for example, the ideas of the Enlightenment are still very important. It is currently being said that 'Christa Wolf is retreating into Romanticism'. That is frequently perceived as being anti-Enlightenment.*

Christa Wolf: That is a very undialectical view, both of literary history and of the writer's appreciation of history. Firstly, neither *Sturm und Drang* nor Romanticism – at least early Romanticism – are anti-Enlightenment: they could equally well be seen as branches of the Enlightenment. The young romantics are the post-revolutionary generation. Unlike the Classicists who could carry on living their utopian lives, they had to cope with the fact that the ideas of the French Revolution had not won out and had not been imported into Germany. Secondly, my work contains no anti-Enlightenment polemic. If I polemicize, then it is against the unchallenged rule of reason and science as this developed in the nineteenth century. Positivism and pure rationalism are the basic causes of the steps we have taken down the path towards the imminent threat of war. The main aim of my work in recent years has been to tackle the question of what it is that has brought our civilization to the brink of self-destruction. One of the causes is the complete exclusion of everything non-rational from what is perceived as progress. I don't call this 'the irrational' because that has such negative overtones in German. As long as technical progress is considered to be the highest value of civilization, which I feel particularly keenly here in America, I can't foresee any possibility of change.

Henry Schmidt: *We should distinguish between the Enlightenment in a historical sense and enlightenment as it affects contemporary readers.*

Christa Wolf: Yes, the last person to take up the banner of the Enlightenment in a positive sense was probably Brecht. But at the time we were students, Brecht was being criticised by Marxist literary theorists.

Helen Fehervary: *From a Lukácsian standpoint?*

Gerhard Wolf: Yes, and by those who had just done new research into the social history of the classical period and had turned Goethe into a great social critic.

Helen Fehervary: *But that was a conservative tendency.*

Christa Wolf: Yes, but for us these seminars also contained much that was progressive, for example getting to know the *Sturm und Drang*. Then it was *Sturm und Drang*, not Romanticism, which for a long time was the literary model for me. Romanticism, as it was presented to us, seemed equally conservative, because I had no first-hand knowledge of it. For a long time it was the young Goethe whom I looked to, his poems and his *Werther*. After that I developed a positive attitude towards Brecht. Only much later did I realize that, as a writer, Brecht had no influence on me whatsoever, and that I had never arrived at a critical judgement on him, either positive or negative, which I suppose in itself is a sort of judgement.

Henry Schmidt: *You only write prose. Why don't you write poetry or drama?*

Christa Wolf: I've found I express myself most naturally in prose. Verse does not flow naturally from me. I have no lyrical talent.

Henry Schmidt: *Why do women in general rarely write plays?*

Christa Wolf: It has to do with the problem of producing the characters from inside yourself, then objectifying them completely and fitting them into a construction.

Helen Fehervary: *Drama has a direct relation to the state.*

Christa Wolf: It is highly institutionalized. You would have to be able to break through that.

Gerhard Wolf: A possible modern medium would be film, but you'd have to be the director yourself, though, the real creator of the characters.

Christa Wolf: Yes, film would interest me.

Henry Schmidt: *As you already have a wide influence, do you feel obliged to write as an example for others, especially for other women writers? Do you sometimes feel inhibited by this responsibility, by the fact that you have already become, so to speak, a classic author?*

Christa Wolf: No, I think it is quite mistaken to suggest that I have already become a classic author. I feel that I am only at the start. I'm not being modest, I really think that first I must formulate what is important for me. When I have formulated something, I always feel that I have planned a definite period of my development. I know perfectly well, then, that very soon it will feel like a strange skin which I will have to tear off both from the inside and the outside. What I am trying to say is that everything I write is provisional. To this extent, I don't see myself as a model for others. In recent years I have found that in discussions with other women writers I am learning or absorbing just as much from them as they are from me. The great danger, less common amongst women who write than amongst women in general, is that they may be seeking a myth or a mother figure and that they latch onto me as that figure. This is an awkward situation and is quite harmful to both parties. I try to avoid it. The power to influence which literature exudes is something I simply try to ignore.

Helen Fehervary: *But in very concrete terms, as far as women as readers are concerned, women do not relate in the same way to the literary heritage as men. Women have a real need for literature. In this feeling that someone is communicating women's experience there is an expression of a real material interest.*

Christa Wolf: That is the positive side of the matter, but there is a restricting side too, in that they are also trying to tie you down and find perfection in either what you write or who you are. This need can be explained historically, but that does not make it productive.

Helen Fehervary: *Why is it that it is Christa Wolf, an East German writer, who is performing a 'pan-German' function?*

Henry Schmidt: *Is it simply a matter of chance?*

Christa Wolf: The remarkable thing about us Germans after the war is that we all acquired a double existence: one in the country in which we were born and one in the country in which we ended up, often by chance. For we belong to the six to twelve million who were resettled from the previously German, now Polish territories. Where these people ended up was at first a matter of pure luck. They tended to go to the West, but many simply got caught in the region to the east of the Elbe. My family and I stayed there and, once I began to develop an interest in politics, I didn't want to leave anyway. Nevertheless each of us has a second possible life story. Gerhard, who at the end of the war was in an area which is now West German, could have stayed on there, although he is from Thuringia. If he had, then his biography would read differently. I could have crossed the Elbe and my life would have taken a completely different course. You have to understand what it means to have grown up under fascism, to then express in writing everything that was destroyed for you in your childhood, to undergo the slow and painful process of letting this grow in you again. Our generation no longer took – nor could take – history and its catastrophes lightly. I know that my compulsion to write is partially a result of wrestling with the GDR problem. This creates a powerful friction; it releases very sharp conflicts and also, clearly, great creative energies.

Gerhard Wolf: Writers are much more conscious of this friction because it is much more direct.

Christa Wolf: What course things would have taken in West Germany, what kind of friction would have led me to write there, I'm not sure. As to how far my life in the GDR predestined me to express something which people in West Germany can also relate to, I don't know either. Other writers, like Sarah Kirsch for example, who left the GDR are also understood in both halves of Germany. We East Germans had a vision, a utopia . . .

Gerhard Wolf: . . . and from this clash between utopia and reality . . .

Christa Wolf: . . . you get some very nice sparks. If you are not destroyed by it, it produces sparks of creativity.

Susanne Pongratz: *Could one say that women in the GDR and West Germany share a similar range of experience because from their perspective the two systems are more alike?*

Christa Wolf: No, it is precisely the experience of women which diverges so widely between the two countries. The systems are alike in so far as both societies are patriarchal. But in the GDR the generation of women to which I belong has, from the beginning, been included on an equal basis in the process of reconstruction. That was a task which we could fulfil as well as men. Although we had to work like mad, to us it seemed worthwhile and only over the last ten years or so have we begun to ask ourselves whether this is actually what we want. But that shows a certain level of economic development is necessary before such questions arise. The fact that economic and legal equality is embedded in law made the development and self-awareness of women in the GDR and West Germany very different. After 1968, the way the West German women's movement voiced their demands began in its turn to exert a very strong influence on women intellectuals in the GDR and raised questions which we had not yet asked. It seems to me, however unqualified I may be to judge, that part of the inner uncertainty of American women, even those who are highly successful, stems from this lack of economic equality. This is absolutely indispensable before women can formulate their own questions.

Henry Schmidt: *But some women begin to lose all interest in these questions once the economic base has been created, because conforming becomes the most important thing.*

Christa Wolf: Yes, the pressure to conform is very great. In the fifties and sixties we went through the same thing. Today, women want to be really different from men and they pose extremely awkward questions for male society, to which it can only react defensively. Men employ a whole range of devices, from insults and ridicule to the direct suppression of what we say, devices which they have constantly employed to try to make women look ridiculous. That is simply something we have to reckon with.

Susanne Pongratz: *As regards the influence of the Western women's movement on the GDR, in what way is it discussed?*

Christa Wolf: It is discussed very little, really. It is talked about in women's discussion groups. The letters I get from my readers suggest that there are lots of such groups. Women who you would not expect to, either because of their age or milieu, suddenly reveal a sensibility for things they find in my books.

Helen Fehervary: *Very little is known here about the influence of your books in the GDR.*

Christa Wolf: The most recent books, since *Christa T.*, have not had much attention from the media in the GDR, though they have been discussed at length in public readings, semi-official events, and in private circles. Their influence often runs beneath the surface. It is very powerful; I have never had cause to complain about a lack of response. For this reason, even in the periods when I was not receiving much media attention, I never felt any sense of isolation.

May 1983

9

THE ORIGINS OF NARRATION

A Conversation with Jacqueline Grenz*

Jacqueline Grenz: *With the novel* Cassandra *and the four Frankfurt lectures* Conditions Of A Narrative, *you lay out around the subject of* Cassandra *a complex which contains elements of both prose and essay writing. The same kind of parallelism was already evident in* The Quest for Christa T. *and the essay* The Reader and the Writer *and again in* No Place On Earth *and the text on Karoline von Günderrode. In* A Model Childhood, *by contrast, the essayistic elements – in the form of reflections on the difficulties of 'describing the workings of memory' – had, to a certain extent, been integrated into the novel. Why, in the case of the Cassandra material, did you return to this parallelism? How do you think your lectures and narratives relate to one another?*

What prompted me to write the *Conditions Of A Narrative* was a request from the University of Frankfurt-am-Main to give a series of lectures on poetics. Before me, authors like Heinrich Böll or Ingeborg Bachmann had spoken there in the sixties and then, after a short gap, at the beginning of the seventies writers like Adolf Muschg, Peter Bichsel, Günter Kunert, Wolfgang Koeppen. The enterprise goes by the name of 'Lectures On Poetics', but poetics was not what I was offering. Since I was working on the Cassandra material at the time, it was a perfect opportunity consciously to monitor the genesis of this narrative in a somewhat more precise way than I would otherwise have done. I was able to pay attention to the various phases of development of the subject matter, of the material, of my own thoughts too. Otherwise much of it disappears again into the unconscious. And despite this, the four lectures subsequently published are but the tip of the iceberg, merely what crystallized out of the

*First published in *Connaissance de la RDA* (Paris), no. 17, December 1983.

process, mere fragments of what this subject matter actually stirred up within me. But they were perhaps important because there was even more material to get to grips with than in *A Model Childhood*.

Jacqueline Grenz: *In the third lecture, which takes the form of a working journal, there is one entry which reads as follows*: 'Meteln, 21st July 1981: Narrative techniques, which in their respective closure or openess also convey patterns of thought. I feel the closed nature of the form of the Cassandra story to be in contradiction with the fragmentary structure in which I see it as really originating. The contradiction cannot be resolved; it can only be acknowledged'* *This filled my head with questions: which narrative techniques do you have in mind here? What thought patterns do they convey? What do you mean by the 'closed form' of the Cassandra story?*

What has emerged as 'narration' in western literature is, I think, only one of a number of possible ways in which an event or a series of experiences can be communicated. We have simply got used to this Homeric form of narration, with its beginning, climax and end and all the corresponding twists and turns, with the ways the lives of the characters unfold and, recently also, with the corresponding psychology. This story, however, was not conceived in this way. I didn't see it as a complete and unified story but as a pattern, a tissue, and I was aware of the fact that in this case I would have to abandon linear narration. This is very difficult, though, because narration takes place within time and time itself has a linear structure. To put it another way: it is not possible to convey this tissue form, all these simultaneous threads that produce a single pattern, through narration, for we narrate things in sequence, one after another. But this is nothing new.

That is one point. The other point concerns the unity of events, or whether one uses events as the starting point at all. Whether one prefers to start from the experience of a certain person or from the experiences which a group of people have through and with each other. For this, an event – here for example the Trojan War – can be a help, but it is certainly not absolutely necessary. It is not the most important thing. But if it's there, it tends to push the organization of the material in the direction of a certain closure. On the other hand, the structure of the lectures, in which I experiment with different things which do not correspond to the story, helps to force open this closed form. The language and the rhythm of the story have emerged from the writing in what becomes an increasingly compelling process. This kind of story is apparently more self-contained

* *Cassandra*, trans. Jan van Heurck, London 1984, p. 266.

than any other form of narration. But for anyone who recognizes that the lectures and the story together form an aesthetic whole, then I think no sense of 'closure' can emerge.

Jacqueline Grenz: *One thing that I find remarkable is that at the very moment that one 'is left speechless', or 'should be left speechless', as you put it in your speech in acceptance of the Büchner Prize, there emerges a construction of linguistic perfection, which creates an impression for me of this very 'closure'. This seems even clearer when I think of* No Place On Earth, *throughout which one has a sense of something left unsaid, the difficulty of communication. This goes for* A Model Childhood *too. In both, as I understand it, it is the difficulty of expressing oneself which is the theme. This difficulty of speaking is evidently absent from* Cassandra. *Is this part of this same contradiction?*

Perhaps that is a part of it. I have never thought that Cassandra should find it difficult to express what she has experienced. This is not where her problem lies. It is that she cannot *act*. Expressing why she cannot act, though, is something she is certainly capable of. At the end of her life, she is able to gather her experience like ripe fruit. This, by the way, is why I don't see her as having failed. Her intention is to retain her consciousness until the very end, and that means that she can formulate her thoughts, for without this, there is no consciousness. I have never seen any problem in that. I know people who have experienced similar things, or worse, and who, after a certain time, have been able to express their experience. I don't think there is a fundamental difficulty here. No doubt one can be silent, one can become speechless. Cassandra is silent too. She doesn't speak. . . .

Jacqueline Grenz: *She doesn't speak to anybody else. . . .*

She doesn't speak out loud, she *thinks*. Nor would I allow her to speak, that would be inconceivable, impossible. But I can certainly let her think, reflect on her experiences. Or to put it more accurately: the thoughts go on inside her, and she can't switch them off, even if she wanted to. I think there is a big difference here.

Jacqueline Grenz: *Her inner monologue, though, is highly structured.*

It is not a naturalistic monologue. I gave it an organization, as one must with any material, because otherwise it just remains 'raw material'. You can get some sense of the difference between material that has been structured and material that hasn't if you compare the lectures and the story. In the lectures, I have sometimes written down the story completely bare, as fact. In the story it is then 'organized. There's not much I can say about this. It's no longer under my control and I can no longer alter it. I can only say: this is how it developed. Later you can only reflect on it. Perhaps you need more form, more organization, when the subject matter itself is particularly harrowing. *No Place On Earth* is, I feel, highly organized. I couldn't have written it if it hadn't been – perhaps that is an explanation. Form is always at the same time a protection against the 'disorganization', the wildness, the destructiveness of conflicts, which must emerge and be expressed on the material. And something that the reader can demand: the elimination of purely chance elements.

Jacqueline Grenz: *In* A Model Childhood, *strangely enough, exactly in the place where Charlotte turns into a 'Cassandra behind a shop counter' one finds the comment:* 'Form as a possibility of gaining distance. Forms of gaining distance, which are never accidental, never arbitrary '* *Could one say that the form of the Cassandra story arrives at a kind of closed perfection because precisely with such subject material, it was necessary to gain a degree of detachment?*

I think it has something to do with that. But I don't think that the form of the Cassandra story is as 'perfect' as you feel it is. Every time I read it, I know where the gaps are, where things have been left unexplained, where something has been left open or passed over in silence. An example of this is the relationship between Cassandra and Aeneas, or perhaps more so the structures which emerge between the women in the mountains. Where utopian elements come in, nothing is closed off, nothing is brought to a conclusion. Behind what is written, there is the glimmer of an alternative existence.

Jacqueline Grenz: *Is Panthous one of the characters who is not fully developed?*

Panthous remains an enigma to Cassandra. She cannot see through him entirely. He represents for her the enigma of the contradiction between superiority and arrogance on the one hand, and helplessness on the other. The relationship between Cassandra and Panthous is ambivalent; nothing is completely resolved. This is intentional, it is left to speak for itself. As far as Aeneas is concerned, though, he is more of an outline, a sketch. He doesn't appear much and has little opportunity to develop as a character, to become rounded. He remains an outline whilst the motivations of other

---

* *A Model Childhood*, trans. Farrar Straus and Giroux Inc., London 1980, p. 164.

characters – Polyxena, for example – are made more explicit, and it is much clearer why they act and react in certain ways. Much more is taken for granted in Aeneas, so much more is left open. The narrator fears certain characters and relationships. As in every story, there is a hierarchy of characters, running from those who are drawn in detail down – disappearing more and more into the shadows – to those who are on the periphery, who possibly put in only a single appearance. This is a necessary economy of narration. If you could narrate as a painter paints, so that you grasp the whole tableau at one glance, then all the characters would be equal. But you would not have their behaviour, their development. You have to confront the choice between the two possibilities presented in narration. This is something which is becoming increasingly problematic for me. I cannot make my mind up to produce simultaneity artificially through certain forms, like for example a documentary collage. This would have been completely inconceivable for this kind of subject matter. There are elements of this in the lectures, though, and I admit the story would look different if it were not accompanied by the lectures. This is no doubt difficult for readers and critics to realize.

Jacqueline Grenz: *In the third lecture you say*: 'I will need much more time for the story, which I increasingly see as a *roman à clef*, than I had anticipated for the didactic tale which I must originally have had in mind.'* *If you intend to write a didactic tale, you not only want to raise questions but, from the outset, you have to have the answers to these questions ready, solutions to be communicated, more or less explicitly, to the readers or audience through the narrative in order to convince them. Yet the finished work seems to me to betray rather the opposite attitude.*

It developed into the opposite attitude. At the beginning, I really did only know the bare facts which everybody knows when they hear the name Cassandra. She was the Trojan woman who prophesied to the inhabitants of Troy that their city would be destroyed and whom no-one believed. From this, you could derive the simple message: people who 'know' and predict the fate of others, are never believed. It could have been a *roman à thèse* or didactic piece. But through the knowledge I gained about early history and the environment in which Cassandra might have lived, I came to write something totally different. When I saw Mycenae and Crete I was able to imagine the landscapes she lived in. It wasn't Asia Minor but it was the same kind of air, sky and stone as the landscape she would have lived in. This profound sensory experience overturned the didactic idea. The fact that she was a seer whom nobody believed became less and less

Cassandra, p.264 [translation modified here].

important and, in fact, it is now barely mentioned in the story. What I then wrote is not a parable. More than anything, it is perhaps an experiment with a model. The story is not intended to prove something, not even something complex. The figure of Cassandra interested me, her contradictoriness fascinated me too much for that.

Jacqueline Grenz: *If one thinks of Wilhelm Girnus's caustic comments in his article in* Sinn und Form *(no. 2, 1983), you can nonetheless see the danger that the story may be already transposed into the present. Wouldn't you agree?*

Wilhelm Girnus did not 'transpose' it into the present. The subject matter already has great significance for the present. At least I hope that the lectures and story together are very relevant today. He attacked the fourth lecture, which was published in *Sinn und Form*. Apart from the criticism of supposed mistakes in my perception of history and of linguistic diversions, his main objection is that I repress or rather ignore class contradictions in order to present the primary contradictions as that between the sexes. This he denounces. Both men and women have often reacted anxiously or defensively to the real emancipation of women, which has only just begun, and which is still going on even in the GDR. I think this is one such reaction, in written form. You often encounter deliberate, malicious misunderstanding, though sometimes you simply meet unconscious defences, the fear of the possibility of criticism or of demands which will not be of benefit to oneself. Who ever gives up their privileges without a fight? People are much more likely to use all kinds of excuses and mount counter-attacks.

Jacqueline Grenz: *The tone of Girnus's article is exceptionally acerbic. It seems to me that you could conclude from this vehemence that the author is not only reacting against the question of women's liberation, but against something much more sensitive: the breaking of a taboo. In this book, you questioned the unchallenged rule of optimism, and in my opinion this explains the almost abusive reaction. In a way, this reminds me of the reaction to* Christa T., *a book whose theme, death, was also taboo, and still largely remains so.*

Perhaps it was taboo then. In the last ten or fifteen years, though, there have been developments within literature, and it is now a seismograph for what is going on in society. Of course, there are profound reasons why a society represses thoughts of death. But in the GDR, we now write and talk about it: the subject is no longer entirely taboo.

Jacqueline Grenz: *But at the time it was – and I think that in* A Model Childhood *you broke a further taboo, that of having come to terms with the past completely. So, once again, there were very bitter reactions.*

It bothered some people that those who lived in Germany in the Nazi period were not portrayed in black and white terms. In this case I don't think it is a question of 'coming to terms'. We have only 'come to terms' with this period in so far as we have discovered the social causes of fascism. Everybody now knows what led to fascism and I see no danger of the re-emergence of fascism as a socio-economic phenomenon in our country. On the other hand, we live daily with people who were alive at that time and still carry with them the extremely traumatic experiences of the period, whether as victims or collaborators. It is the trauma of the victims of the persecution which is always the stronger. I ask, why? Yes, it is true, my book touched on national traumas and, inevitably, it opened up old wounds.

With my first books, I didn't understand why certain people misconstrued them and then reacted very strongly to what they had misconstrued. This phenomenon was repeated several times and gradually I realized that these books obviously caused pain to certain people – and to different people each time. One reaction I met with was a denying of the facts; another, 'deliberate' misunderstanding; a third, slandering the author. In this century, too much has built up in German families and institutions which people would like not to talk or even think about. One cannot in this century create literature without breaking taboos, at least not in the two German states, and I assume elsewhere too. Of course, I don't sit down at the typewriter, every time I tackle a new subject, with the intention of offending anybody. No, I want to make *myself* aware of the things which offend and hurt me, of my own inner taboos and conflicts. Before the violent reaction from outside arose, I had to go through my own violent reaction. Like my readers, I am split.

The defensive reaction in the case of *Cassandra* appears to be directed towards my attempt to express in a forthright manner how I see our situation and the European situation in general. On the other hand, I know hardly anybody in this country who is constantly optimistic about the future, who does not think about, is not profoundly worried about, the position the world – and especially Europe, our own country included – finds itself in. It is hard to make the next step and ask why civilisation is in this state. The fact that the book will be published, this autumn, in the GDR, shows it is possible to express this fear and concern.

Jacqueline Grenz: *In* A Model Childhood, *you said:* 'On what grounds can you suppress this suspicion: whether the fact that during the last couple of years you have anticipated catastrophes less and less – confirming that the postwar era is drawing to a close – whether this has influenced the choice of your subject matter.'* *Is* Cassandra, *by contrast, a book which was written in a 'pre-war atmosphere'?*

Personally, I feel that we have had only a very short period of inner relief, of being free of the depression and oppression of feeling threatened. These threats have grown in the last six years, and particularly in the last two years. I am not alone in feeling this: many other people feel the same way, and not only intellectuals. In the lectures, I say Hitler has caught up with us. What I mean by that is that what he didn't quite manage to do, we may well succeed in doing ourselves. It may be that a kind of thinking has remained in the world, which, though it did not begin in the Third Reich, certainly found its most destructive expression there. It could be that apparently pure instrumental thinking, which in fact totally confuses means and ends, and may complete the job of total destruction. So this whole century may stand under a particularly sinister sign, one we cannot yet see simply because we are still too close to it, and which we try to wriggle away from when we sense it approaching.

Literature cannot fend this off with any certainty. It will probably not be able to change anything. But it has at least to articulate what so many people are feeling; it has at least to support them in their fear and their depression, and of course in their efforts at self-defence, because otherwise they would feel very much alone. I think it is important to articulate positions of resistance. Today, the advent of the peace movement in West Germany, for example, has changed things quite a lot in this respect, though for a while it really looked as if the members of that movement were actually 'mad'. It often happens that those who are possessed by crazed thinking label all those who do not adhere to their delusion mad. The highly dangerous moment we now face – by 'moment' I don't mean an instant, but nevertheless a relatively short period of time – has emerged through an interlacing of many threads of history. . . .

Jacqueline Grenz: *In the face of which, many are filled with a sense of powerlessness. Many wonder if nuclear catastrophe is avoidable at all. . . .*

I don't think it is unavoidable. I see hope in the sense in which Brecht expresses it in one of his poems in the *Buckow Elegies*: 'We'll be done for, unless . . .'. The poem goes:

---

* A Model Childhood, p. 93.

Friends, I'd like you to know the truth and speak it.
Not like tired, evasive Caesars: 'Tomorrow grain will come'
But like Lenin: By tomorrow
We'll be done for, unless ...
As the jingle has it:
Brothers, my first obligation
Is to tell you outright:
We're in a tough situation
With no hope in sight
Friends, a wholehearted admission
And a wholehearted UNLESS!*

If we have ever been in this position, then we certainly are today. The situation is hopeless if large sections of our societies do not introduce new scales of values, if they do not abandon this attitude of *higher, faster, better!* If quite different values are not given priority, if we don't recognize that it is useless to oppose weapons systems with weapons systems, if we don't recognize that a new way must be sought between the false alternatives.... This is of course difficult for our side when we face the Reagan administration on the other, but, nevertheless, it is imperative. We must begin from where we are ourselves. It seems to me that the point to which Western civilisation has brought itself in its hierarchical, patriarchal, class-ridden existence has its own terrible logic, which one can only escape if one cuts through it. In the younger generation I see people – I don't know if there are enough of them – who are willing to do this, even if it means sacrificing their own consumption, prosperity and high-technology. But I don't know if we have enough time left for them to have an influence on events.

Jacqueline Grenz: *When you say 'hierarchical, patriarchal, class-ridden', do you place particular emphasis on the word 'patriarchal'?*

Patriarchy emerged with class society and private ownership of the means of production. If half the inhabitants of the Western world, namely women, for centuries if not for millennia, have not been able to contribute at all to official structures, have not been able to determine anything, not even their own lives, but have rather themselves been re-shaped in the direction of merely functioning rather than thinking and feeling – then this must have certain consequences. I am convinced that these conditions have had and still do have great effects. The transition to patriarchy significantly reshaped the structures of society.

*From 'The Truth Unites', trans. Derek Bowman, in John Willett and Ralph Manheim (eds.), *Bertolt Brecht, Poems 1913-56*, London 1976, p. 441.

Jacqueline Grenz: *When one talks about specifically female characteristics, and those which are lacking in the 'male world' – you use the expression yourself in the lectures – the question then arises as to whether these characteristics are present from birth....*

They are, of course, historically developed characteristics. My position is a long way from biological essentialism. I have tried to proceed historically within early history, of which we have little certain knowledge. I am a long way from idealising 'women' or 'the feminine'.... But apart from that, as a woman myself, I place myself as a Marxist plainly on the side of the oppressed and I do not let myself be persuaded that oppression is good or can be useful, and I include in this the oppression of women by men.

Jacqueline Grenz: *In* Cassandra, *there is the character Penthesilea who rebels against the 'male world'. How do you see her?*

With Penthesilea – who is an interesting phenomenon, and not only in Kleist's famous play – I tried to show an evolution. I wanted to show how this obsession with femininity can go astray. It embodies a sectarian tendency which I find repugnant, as I do everything which amounts to purely separating off those different from oneself and behaving in a hostile manner towards them. This is how I interpret the Penthesilea position. I was interested less in Penthesilea than in those women who were prepared to analyze their own position, who didn't rush into an absolute battle against men and the male world, but who were able to put themselves in question too. Their position is more productive because it does not break the connections with society as a whole.

Jacqueline Grenz: *You write that your investigation of the background to the story produces a new visual grid. In the introduction, there is a sentence which, I think, is connected with this new visual grid, but which remains a mystery to me (probably because it is apparently diametrically opposed to the conception of art as a possible route towards humanization). You say: 'There is and there can be no poetics which prevents the living experience of countless perceiving subjects from being killed and buried in art objects. So does this mean that art objects ("works") are products of the alienation of our culture, whose other finished products are produced for self-annihilation?'* How are we to understand these lines?*

These lines don't say anything new. An art object, which one may greatly admire, has always been selected from the great number of possibilities on

---

* *Cassandra*, p. 142.

offer, and therefore it has pushed out other objects. In industrial societies, in which the art objects I am talking about here originated and continue to be produced, this merciless selection process is constantly taking place. This is simply because the practice of art is a privilege. The situation is different, for example, in societies where ritual still exists, or the practice of art in common – if not in a particularly sophisticated way – in a village community or tribe. In art as it has developed in Europe, though – and in saying this, I am not trying to make it out to be superior in any way – this selection plays an undeniable role. One person speaks, the other is silent. Because one person is silent, the other can, must speak. By so doing, does the latter intensify the silence of the former? The problem is not a moral one. It would be foolish to let this become a question of guilt. Nevertheless, the question is there and, as a writer, I cannot avoid asking it. I do not know if this situation can be changed. Within this mode of production, certainly not. It was precisely while I was concerned with Homer and the classical authors, who have buried a great deal under their great monumental poetry – whole peoples, whole regions, whole social structures and their myths – that I was more and more pressingly made aware of these facts. As these authors formulated so perfectly what was important to them – and it would be absurd to want to 'reproach' them for this – they suppressed everything else, they let everything else slide into oblivion. Before me stood Greek antiquity. And Aeschylus in his *Oresteia*, for example, must destroy the moral commandment that the rights of the mother have precedence over the rights of the father. He must install patriarchy. Fundamentally, though, every literature destroys in the sense that it preaches its own morality and declares all preceding or competing moral standards to be inferior.

At the point in history at which we now find ourselves, I think it is vitally important that we incorporate as many of the experiences of our contemporaries as possible into our thinking and writing, instead of fending them off, declaring them to be inferior or even diabolic, or suppressing them through silence. At the very least, we must regard them as worthy interlocutors and not disqualify or disparage them. As a rule, you don't notice when you are adopting this arrogant, let's say Eurocentric attitude. It is not until – or, rather, may not be until – you come into contact with other cultures that you wake up and come to live less securely, because in other cultures other values prevail, which show you your own are only relative. It cannot be wrong, I think, for literature always to provoke the moral standards of its own culture or civilisation a little. Moreover, this is something which fosters peace....

Jacqueline Grenz: *Has this provocation been intensified by the encounter with Minoan culture, which you came across in your work on* Cassandra?

The encounter with Minoan culture on my trip to Greece was an experience which shocked me. But this sense of alienation can, to a greater or lesser degree, be experienced if you travel, as I did for example this spring, to the USA, or, in the other direction, to the Soviet Union, or to one of the Asiatic countries. You can already feel your own values waver when you travel to countries which are very near but merely lie on a different latitude.

Jacqueline Grenz: *I would like to touch on one final topic. It seems to me that a general theme of your books since* The Quest For Christa T. *would be remembering. That theme was treated directly in* A Model Childhood, *but it seems to me that it plays a large part in other books too.*

Reminding, remembering and narrating are closely bound together. One reason for the emergence of narration, if we look at it historically, is that the members of society – I am thinking again here of the Homeridae, for example – needed to feel remembered, or to be reminded of their long past history. The recalling of history and stories in order to make the village, tribal, or national community aware of its own origin and development has always been a function of narration. In spite of all the other forms of media which have taken away from narration, this function of remembering and chronicling an aspect of that original meaning remains in our modern narrative, though admittedly other tasks have devolved upon it. . . .

   In my books remembering is sometimes a structuring element, as it is in *The Quest for Christa T.* and *A Model Childhood*. This indicates that I think loss of memory, by an individual or a whole nation, is dangerous, debilitating. In my later books, *No Place On Earth* and *Cassandra*, I am reminding (myself) of something: of the origins of phenomena of alienation in our civilisation. This has been my central problematic over the last seven years. This last, furthest step back into early history, strange as it may seem, makes it possible for me to feel a way into the future, which is really what I am about when I narrate stories from the past.

Autumn 1983

10

TO MARK THE PUBLICATION OF *CASSANDRA*

A Conversation with Brigitte Zimmermann and Ursula Fröhlich*

Question: *At the Berlin Writers' Conference, you said, in essence, that your work could only speak to a peaceful world. How does the present climate of confrontation and arms stockpiling, and particularly the stationing of American medium-range and rocket-launched missiles in Western Europe, affect your work in practice?*

I think the present state of affairs is extremely dangerous. On a personal level I find it very oppressive and something which intrudes into my daily routine. The fact that missiles will be placed on our soil concerns me greatly too. We are well aware that if there were to be a military confrontation, nobody and nothing would remain of the areas in which rockets were stationed. I constantly ask myself whether our country, both German nations, even the whole of central Europe, would survive at all. That influences my writing and my life, my view of daily events and my contact with other people – my children, my grandchildren. They become more precious to me.

Nevertheless, I keep on writing. I don't believe that literature has a crucial influence on major political decisions. But there is also the remarkable psychological mechanism which pushes threatening ideas to the back of your mind and cushions you from them; there is the tenacity of hope. I write with this hope in mind. I try to trace the roots of the contradictions in which our civilization is now entrapped. This is what I was doing in the Cassandra book. That work is very much a product of its time. I do think, incidentally, that it does matter whether one uses one's time productively or idles it away, and under what circumstances too.

*First published in *Wochenpost* (Berlin, GDR), 10 February 1984, as 'Das starke Gefühl gebraucht zu werden'.

Question: *You have said that it is not the role of literature to play any great part in major political events. On the other hand, you also told us how widely* Cassandra *has been used by peace campaigners in West Germany, for example, how they have adopted slogans from it and so on. Isn't that a very important point, the enormous breadth which the peace movement has gained?*

Yes, I accept that, and I'm aware too that it is at times when popular movements are in gestation, or are already gathering momentum, that literature can have a direct impact on events. The fact that young readers in West Germany write to tell me that, as a result of reading *Cassandra*, they are now going to join the peace movement too, is an example of this. But, as a rule, literature has an indirect effect, in that it gradually makes the reader's conception and view of the world more sophisticated and, where possible, transforms it. I have experienced this myself. It was a very long time before books and I read very many books – brought about a profound change in my world-view. The change that is effected may be a very fundamental one and I do definitely see literature as an instrument of change. Nevertheless, such changes can take years and I am plagued by the thought that we don't have much time left, that in fact we have to come up with a new way of thinking very quickly. It is this blade of time hanging over us that motivates my work.

Question: *Is your attitude to the current situation influenced by the belief that good writers are in fact a kind of moral authority whose reactions can be very important to others?*

I am less aware of this when I am writing than, for example, when I am giving this kind of interview. Just glancing at my mail, it would be impossible for me to deny that the writer can become a moral authority these days. This can also be attributed to the absence of – or a change in the role of – other moral authorities. Every time one faces new material, though, one's awareness of being an authority completely evaporates. Every time, the same doubt arises, the fear that I cannot do it justice, as if I had never written before. Each of us must cope with the role of 'moral authority' as well and as honestly as we can. This demands qualities other than those required of someone who is simply a writer, by the way.

Question: *In the spring of last year you and your husband went to the USA for a series of lectures. No doubt, other things were discussed at these apart from literature. Were you able to gain an impression of American politics from the inside?*

An impression, yes. Quite an informed one too, I think. But in just seven weeks I can't claim to have been able to form a complete picture.

We got to know a great number of young people – and some who were not so young – mainly in the academic world, who are suffering under Reaganism. Not all these people were in a position to analyze the roots of these policies or their own suffering. Those who could, and who had formed peace groups – the women in New York for example, who spent the summer campaigning at US missile bases – we admired unreservedly. Their courage is impressive. I have come across this kind of person in the West German peace movement and amongst young people in my own country. They are open and critical, immune from intimidation and incorruptible by career or money, free of angst and pleasure-loving. It is this kind of person that those in power there fear, because they represent an alternative vision of the future. We would feel immediately at home amongst them.

But we also got to know people within the establishment: a Democratic Governor and his wife, for example, who were sincerely worried about the implications of Reaganite politics. They genuinely wanted to know something about the impulse behind the European peace movement and its development. We met people who, in our conversations, really were seeking non-Reaganite answers to the internal problems besetting the USA.

For the press and the public in the USA, Europe is a very distant, little known continent. This lack of knowledge leaves the way open for myth, particularly when such a large part of the population consists of first, second or third generation immigrants. Amongst them are people who have fled from soul-destroying poverty in their country of origin – in Mexico or Puerto Rico, for example – and for a long time they wish to do little other, and can do little other, than conform completely to their new environment. One cannot expect this great mass of people to have developed a critical consciousness. This is also true of the frightened middle classes, for whose consumption, I think, myths such as the 'communist menace' are fashioned. Literature can be effective against this. But who reads literature nowadays?

Question: *You were born in 1929, so you belong to a generation which has lived through many different eras. You can still remember the horrors of fascism. Your student days and early working life coincided with the GDR's first attempts to stand on its own feet, a phase which marks a new beginning in German history. The books you have published over the last two decades – a steady flow of work – have moved in step with events which have occurred here and are part of greater processes at work in Europe. Could it be said that it was your generation's unique universe of historical experience which made you a writer, and has your motivation changed since then?*

Your question touches on the peculiar field of conflict in which my generation was placed, and on the sort of friction out of which art itself emerges. Yes, it seems to me that in my generation, which has experienced numerous radical social changes, both of these have been particularly acute and from the very beginning I drew my energy to write from this highly charged field. Perhaps no generation will ever be 'put through the mill' as much as ours was: from the almost devastating experience of being turned into the object of history, to the often demanding and even over-demanding nature of the attempt, in the literary world too, to become its subject. My motivation for writing has not changed significantly over the decades, but the accent has shifted. I have become more certain of the fact that my main motive is one of self-exploration. It was always at that point where I discovered something which I previously didn't know, or at least had been unable to articulate, about my relationship to my own time, to its currents and institutions, and to my contemporaries, or to myself, that an excitement and a feeling of authenticity appeared. And it is this feeling, this sense of alarm at finding that reality is not a creation external to us, but a process which we are subject to and yet which we at the same time bring about ourselves, which really prompts me to write. This is what I see as being productive.

Had I lived at another place and in another time, I would probably have felt the same compulsion to write, because it is part of my personality. Whether it would have been so intense, as it has been in tackling the problems and conflicts I am confronted with by life in the GDR, I don't know. Whether the same quasi-fanaticism about these experiences, problems and conflicts or this imaginary, uninterrupted conversation, which is often closer to a dispute or an argument with the people I live with, would have emerged anywhere else, I don't know.

Question: *In what you say about your generation, as well as what you have written about yourself and your age-group, for example in* A Model Childhood, *you judge it very harshly. Perhaps that is part of your job. But surely the members of that generation should not constantly have to apologize for their existence? In the final analysis, it was they who were crucial in making our state what it is today.*

Harsh? Do you think so? I think that the novel about my generation has yet to be written. If it were, it would not have anything to do with glossing over things or excusing anybody, but would be a sober analysis, which would be painful, especially for the person who wrote it. And it would not have to do with measuring the good intentions of hard-working people, but would tackle the question of what this hard work has made these people as human beings. It seems to me that it is we who must ask this question of ourselves. If we don't, our children will.

The assertion that 'society', at this or that moment in time, made this or that mistake, is relatively uninteresting to me in literary terms. I am interested in what I knew, suspected, thought, did or did not do at a particular time. What have I or have we 'forgotten' about it? What has distanced us from ourselves, from our earlier hopes and ideas, and what is worth taking with us into a future, more human life together? This is the real question. In this we – especially we who are people of letters – have a debt of honesty to younger generations.

Question: *Do you see yourself as part of a particular literary tradition?*

Spontaneously I would like to answer 'yes', but I know I would find the next question – 'Which one?' – difficult to answer. My early development as a writer would have been inconceivable without having known and intensively absorbed the work of the German anti-fascists, the former emigrants, who decisively shaped the self-perceptions of people writing in my generation and whom we, in all modesty, see as our precursors. At that time I was working in the Writers' Union and it was crucial for my development that I was able personally to get to know such a wide variety of people as Fürnberg, Weiskopf, Alex Wedding, and Kuba too, and was able to talk to Uhse, Bredel, Claudius, Hermlin (somewhat later), and Kurt and Jeanne Stern about their lives. I was able, too, to question some of them about their emigration, about Spain, Mexico, the Soviet Union, and to observe them in situations of political conflict. I gradually became friends with some of them and still am. Clichés never lasted long among them. They related their historty, our pre-history, differently, more vividly than text-books ever did. I still remember a great deal of it today, even the circumstances that caused these stories to be told.

To come back to your question about literary tradition in a narrower sense, my relationship with Anna Seghers and my lengthy study of her work occupies a special place. From past German literature, Büchner and Kleist in the field of prose and Thomas Mann are particularly important to me. Then, for a time it was Aragon, Thomas Wolf, the South Americans. An author such as Bulgakov, and his *The Master and Margarita* was very important for me. Tolstoy, Dostoevsky's *The Brothers Karamazov*. Does that cc nstitute a 'tradition'? You read and look at how those who came before you did it, but when you begin to write, all your adopted literary guardians vanish into the background. You don't feel that they even help you with a single sentence, but that is probably not true.

In recent years, women's writing has become a very important literary tradition for me. It would take a work in itself to cover all that could be said on that. The lectures accompanying *Cassandra* deal with it at some length, so I will limit myself here to just a few names: Ingeborg Bachmann, Virginia Woolf, Marie-Luise Fleisser.

Question: *Over a million copies of your books have appeared in the GDR. A Model Childhood alone went into its ninth edition in February. What's more, your work has been translated into twenty languages. Aside from the socialist countries, German-speaking areas and the USA, they have been published in Japan, France, Italy and Scandinavia. You are an important representative of East German literature. How do you cope with that? When you travel outside the socialist bloc, do you find you first have to 'explain' your country before you can talk about literature?*

There are two questions there. I have learned that it is best to be myself – and not to make myself out to be a 'representative' of anything, least of all a 'representative' of myself. Then it is my history, my experience, my view of the world, which comes out. And today it is no longer true that in other countries an East German writer has to 'explain' his or her country first. That is something I experienced very much in the sixties, but today I think people listen more carefully to the nuances in discussions, which are often more likely to reveal any differences than open declarations. . . .

Question: *Differences on your part?*

In my structures of thought, my outlook. This struck me very noticeably in the USA, particularly amongst women. The majority of women there find it difficult to recognize the blind spot, to explode the myth in which their society shrouds itself. The penetrating questions I am asked there and the answers I give, testify to our different social backgrounds.

On the other hand, when I return home I too have a 'new outlook'. I can then see our 'blind spots' much more clearly again. The mechanisms which we find difficult to explode strike me more forcefully. What do we see of ourselves, and what can we perhaps no longer see? I think literature can also reduce the number of 'blind spots', can illuminate them. It is not easy to do this in any country. It is frequently misunderstood or interpreted – to put it mildly – as ill-will.

Question: *Indeed, not everything you have written has been immediately approved, and one or two things you have done, or not done, have run up against opposition here. How do you cope with this in a profession which is dependent on publicity?*

This problem is worth taking a little further. Even if I forget the publisher's reader who wrote to me after the poor reception of *Christa T.*, suggesting that I should give up writing, my opinion on this matter is that for many years critics and theorists here have had an arrogant attitude to contemporary writers and their work. But it is one thing to be aware of that, and quite another to cope with serious personal attacks. In my case this has merely meant I have written one or two books fewer, and reflected more on what I really want to write and feel I have to write.

I accept that literature, if it is worthy of the name, i.e., if it goes beyond the boundaries of everyday thought, can be discomfiting and provoke opposition. With each book I have published, I have seen the public at first divided, but then later, as time passes, the number of readers prepared to take seriously the concerns I engage with increases. Experience and patience are needed – on all sides. In any case, that's what I think at the moment. My lifetime is not unlimited, and I can't be bothered to wear myself out in fruitless squabbling any more. I just want to write now.

Question: *With all due respect, you have proved to be one of those writers who refuse to make it easy for the reader. Your thoughts are mastered only by those who are prepared to comprehend the intellectual adventure which you create as you write. Despite – or perhaps because of – this, your books achieve a large circulation. What has your experience of readers been like here in the GDR? How does the public react to the demands you make on them?*

Writers who work with a certain subject matter for years reach a point – it is impossible not to – when they feel completely at ease with it. They cannot always demand the same of readers, though, especially when (as was the case with *Cassandra* or *No Place On Earth*) a particular cultural heritage is involved, which is no longer accessible. I think I provide some assistance through the lectures which are essential to the Cassandra novel. Basically, though, ever since *The Divided Heaven*, I've been seen as 'difficult'. An unpractised readership had met an unfamiliar literary form. Today, sixteen-year-olds read it without difficulty. Today, readers know the work of the South Americans, Kafka, Proust, Musil, and no longer demand a flat, linear naturalism rather than a narrative style which, precisely for the sake of realism, is slightly more complicated. Today, when I am asked disapprovingly who I am really writing for, then I say, for readers. By that, I mean for people who use literature to extend their own experience and knowledge. I will never manage, however, to transform non-readers into readers. Sometimes, though, I find my book being labelled too difficult by someone who says that he himself understood it but thinks 'ordinary people' will not be able to. Well, if ordinary people now run into hundreds of thousands, then I am quite content.

As regards your last question, I have never come across such a large, sophisticated, demanding – and also grateful – public as in the GDR.

Question: *What are you reading at the moment?*

A book on ethnology. I'm also re-reading Virginia Woolf's *To The Light-house*, which is giving me great pleasure. And *Der Laden* by Strittmatter. Some time ago, I was forced to give up trying to read everything published in the GDR, but I read as many books by women as I can. You can learn a lot from them about everyday life in this country. I have also kept up my interest in books on early history and mythology.

Question: *You are not only a successful, but also an industrious writer. You produce a lot on a quite regular basis. Your world must be a very well-ordered one.*

I do write regularly, but that doesn't mean that I write every day. I have had to learn to accept that my manuscripts will develop very slowly and need numerous experiments and false starts, so it is generally years before the first page is 'done'. You say I am industrious, but I constantly feel I don't work hard enough. When my children were small, it was difficult to organize my writing time strictly. I wasted a lot of time in useless meetings. It was then, I think, that I lost my ability to concentrate for hours on end as I could in my student days. I could work into the night then, and did too. I can't do that any more.

On the other hand, now with a 'well-ordered world' and a strict daily regime I can in theory produce steadily. For example, four hours in the morning and three to four in the afternoon. On good days, that is; in reality, they are rare. An average day tends to consist of a mass of different hold-ups and diversions, which arise from the fact that growing recognition for a writer also increases the number of people who make requests of you, of a professional, personal, or social nature. So there is a lot of post, a lot of telephoning. I'm not complaining. I have learnt to accept this part of my job as well. But sometimes it's a miracle if I can find time for 'real' work. On the other hand, I wouldn't like to miss the intense contact with readers which letters, visits and readings give me. It is this contact which not only brings me a great deal of outside factual information that I could not get in any other way, but of course also gives me a greater feeling of being needed, and when it comes down to it, that is what inspires me to write.

November 1983

BIBLIOGRAPHY

German Editions

This bibliography is taken from Colin E. Smith, *Tradition, Art and Society: Christa Wolf's Prose*. Verlag die blaue Eule, Essen/FRG 1987. This is the only comprehensive work on Wolf available in English, and includes a full bibliographical list.

Moskauer Novelle, Halle 1961; Romanzeitung 204, Berlin/GDR 1966.
Der geteilte Himmel, Halle 1963; Berlin/West 1964; Munich 1973.
Nachdenken über Christa T., Halle 1968 (second edition 1973); Neuwied and Berlin 1969 (paperback 1971).
Lesen und Schreiben. Aufsätze und Betrachtungen (Afterword by Hans Stubbe), Berlin and Weimar 1971 (second, revised edition 1973).
Lesen und Schreiben. Aufsätze und Prosastücke, Darmstadt and Neuwied 1972.
Till Eulenspiegel. Erzählungen für den Film (with Gerhard Wolf), Berlin and Weimar 1972; Darmstadt and Neuwied 1973 (paperback reissue 1982); Frankfurt 1976.
Unter den Linden. Drei unwahrscheinliche Geschichten, Berlin and Weimar 1974; Darmstadt and Neuwied 1974 (paperback of title story only, 1977).
Kindheitsmuster, Berlin and Weimar 1976; Darmstadt and Neuwied 1977 (paperback 1979).
Kein Ort. Nirgends, Berlin and Weimar 1979; Darmstadt and Neuwied 1979 (paperback 1981).
Fortgesetzter Versuch. Aufsätze, Gespräche, Essays, Leipzig 1979 (third, revised edition 1982).
Lesen und Schreiben. Neue Sammlung, Darmstadt and Neuwied 1980 (second, revised edition 1981).
Gesammelte Erzählungen, Darmstadt and Neuwied 1980 (paperback, 1981).
Kassandra. Erzählung, Darmstadt and Neuwied 1983 (paperback, 1986).
Voraussetzungen einer Erzählung: Kassandra. Frankfurter Poetik-Vorlesungen, Darmstadt and Neuwied 1983.
Kassandra. Vier Vorlesungen. Eine Erzählung, Berlin and Weimar 1983 (third lecture shortened).

Erzählungen, Berlin and Weimar 1985.
Ins Ungebundene geht eine Sehnsucht. Gesprächsraum Romantik. Prosa und Essays (with Gerhard Wolf), Berlin and Weimar 1985.
Störfall. Nachrichten eines Tages, Berlin and Weimar 1987; Darmstadt and Neuwied 1987.
Die Dimension des Autors. Essays und Aufsätze, Reden und Gespräche 1959-1985, Berlin and Weimar (two volumes) 1987; Darmstadt and Neuwied 1987.

English Translations

Divided Heaven, transl. by Joan Becker. Seven Seas Books, Berlin 1965 (out of print).
The Reader and Writer. Essays, Sketches, Memories, transl. by Joan Becker. Seven Seas Books, Berlin 1977 (out of print).
The Quest for Christa T., transl. by Christopher Middleton. Virago Press 1982.
A Model Childhood, transl. by Ursula Molinaro and Hedwig Rappold. Virago Press 1983.
No Place on Earth, transl. by Jan van Heurck. Virago Press 1983.
Cassandra. A Novel and Four Essays, transl. by Jan van Heurck. Virago Press 1984.
Accident, transl. by Heike Schwarzbauer. Virago Press 1989.